A COMPANION TO

The Understanding by Design
Guide to Creating High-Quality Units

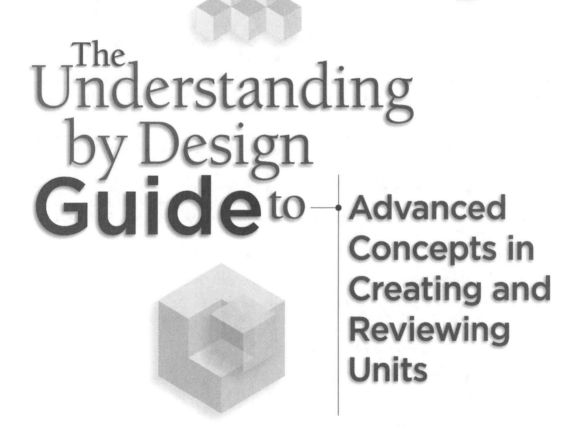

The Understanding by Design Guide to

Advanced Concepts in Creating and Reviewing Units

GRANT WIGGINS AND JAY MCTIGHE

Alexandria, Virginia USA

1703 N. Beauregard St. • Alexandria, VA 22311-1714 USA
Phone: 800-933-2723 or 703-578-9600 • Fax: 703-575-5400
Website: www.ascd.org • E-mail: member@ascd.org
Author guidelines: www.ascd.org/write

Gene R. Carter, *Executive Director*; Ed Milliken, *Chief Program Development Officer*; Carole Hayward, *Publisher*; Julie Houtz, *Director, Book Editing & Production*; Darcie Russell, *Senior Associate Editor*; Georgia Park, *Senior Graphic Designer*; Mike Kalyan, *Production Manager*; Sarah Plumb, *Production Specialist*, Valerie Younkin, *Desktop Publishing Specialist*

© 2012 by Grant Wiggins and Jay McTighe. All rights reserved. It is illegal to reproduce copies of this work in print or electronic format (including reproductions displayed on a secure intranet or stored in a retrieval system or other electronic storage device from which copies can be made or displayed) without the prior written permission of the publisher. By purchasing only authorized electronic or print editions and not participating in or encouraging piracy of copyrighted materials, you support the rights of authors and publishers. Readers who wish to duplicate this copyrighted material may do so for a small fee by contacting the Copyright Clearance Center (CCC), 222 Rosewood Dr., Danvers, MA 01923, USA (phone: 978-750-8400; fax: 978-646-8600; Web: www.copyright.com). For requests to reprint or to inquire about site licensing options, contact ASCD Permissions at www.ascd.org/permissions, or permission@ascd.org, or 703-575-5749. For a list of vendors authorized to license ASCD e-books to institutions, see www.ascd.org/epubs. Send translation inquiries to translations@ascd.org.

Understanding by Design® and UbD™ are trademarks of the Association for Supervision and Curriculum Development. ASCD EDge® is a trademark of the Association for Supervision and Curriculum Development.

Printed in the United States of America. Cover art © 2012 by ASCD. ASCD publications present a variety of viewpoints. The views expressed or implied in this book should not be interpreted as official positions of the Association.

All web links in this book are correct as of the publication date below but may have become inactive or otherwise modified since that time. If you notice a deactivated or changed link, please e-mail books@ascd.org with the words "Link Update" in the subject line. In your message, please specify the web link, the book title, and the page number on which the link appears.

PAPERBACK ISBN: 978-1-4166-1409-8   ASCD product #112026   n3/12

Also available as an e-book (see Books in Print for the ISBNs).

Quantity discounts for the paperback edition only: 10–49 copies, 10%; 50+ copies, 15%; for 1,000 or more copies, call 800-933-2723, ext. 5634, or 703-575-5634. For desk copies: member@ascd.org.

Library of Congress Cataloging-in-Publication Data
Wiggins, Grant P., 1950–
    The Understanding by design guide to advanced concepts in creating and reviewing units / Grant Wiggins and Jay McTighe.
        p. cm.
    Includes bibliographical references.
    ISBN 978-1-4166-1409-8 (pbk. : alk. paper)
    1. Curriculum planning—United States. 2. Curriculum-based assessment—United States. 3. Lesson planning—United States. I. McTighe, Jay. II. Wiggins, Grant P., 1950–Understanding by design. III. Title.
    LB2806.15.W547 2012
    375'.001—dc23
                                                                        2011041515

22 21 20 19 18 17 16 15 14 13 12   1 2 3 4 5 6 7 8 9 10 11 12

CSN LIBRARY

DISCARD

LB
2806.15
.W547
2012

Wiggins, Grant P.,
1950- author.
The understanding
by design guide to
advanced concepts in
creating and
reviewing units

FEB 1 0 2017

The Understanding by Design Guide to

Advanced Concepts in

Creating and Reviewing Units

• • • • •

**Other ASCD books
by Grant Wiggins and Jay McTighe**

Schooling by Design: Mission, Action, and Achievement
Understanding by Design Expanded 2nd Edition
The Understanding by Design Guide to Creating High-Quality Units
Understanding by Design Professional Development Workbook

Note: *The Understanding by Design Guide to Creating High-Quality Units*
is a companion to
The Understanding by Design Guide to Advanced Concepts in Creating and Reviewing Units.

The Understanding by Design Guide to
Advanced Concepts in Creating and Reviewing Units

· · · · ·

List of Figures

The figures critical to exploring Understanding by Design are printed within and page numbers are supplied. Additional figures that may be helpful are available online and are noted with the OO (online only) designation. All figures may be downloaded for your convenience.

Downloads/Key Page

The figures in this book, as well as additional worksheets and examples, are available for download at www.ascd.org/downloads

Enter this unique key code to unlock the files:

GBC45 0FDD5 D2514

If you have difficulty accessing the files, e-mail webhelp@ascd.org or call 1-800-933-ASCD for assistance.

Introduction

The Understanding by Design Guide to Advanced Concepts in Creating and Reviewing Units is targeted to individuals and groups interested in refining their skills in designing units of study based on *The Understanding by Design Guide to Creating High-Quality Units*. This guide is also organized around a set of modules through which designers are guided. Figure 1 offers a graphic representation of the organization of the modules in this volume.

This guide looks more closely at refinements to the unit designs, while also introducing new material on self-assessment, peer review, implementation, and supervision of the unit—under the new headings of Stages 4, 5, and 6.

Each module in both *Guides* includes the following components:

- Narrative discussion of key ideas in the module
- Guiding exercises, worksheets, and design tips for unit design
- An example of an emerging design

Figure 1

Outline of Modules

Stage 1— Desired Results	Stage 2— Assessment Evidence	Stage 3— Learning Plan
Module I: Unpacking Standards	Module J: Identifying Evaluative Criteria for Assessments	Module K: Refining the Learning Plan in Stage 3
Module L: Sharpening Essential Questions and Understandings	Module M: Authentic Assessment and Validity	Module N: Differentiating— Tailoring the Learning Plan to the Learners
Module O: Designing the Lesson Plan for Your Unit		
Module P: Obtaining and Using Feedback		

- Review criteria (design standards) with prompts for self-assessment
- References for further information

In addition to the print format, the *Guide* features online resources correlated to the text. Many of the exercises and worksheets are accessible as downloads in electronic form, as are additional unit examples. The online portion of the *Guide* will allow updates (such as more unit examples and new resources) to be readily accessed.

Users of the *Guide*, especially beginners, are invited to follow the exercises and worksheets to assist them in thinking through the unit design process. However, it is important to always keep the end—a coherent and well-aligned unit plan—in mind. If you find an exercise or worksheet unnecessary, feel free to skip it. Also, think of the exercises and worksheets like the training wheels on a bicycle. Eventually you'll find that you no longer need them as your understanding of UbD deepens and your unit design skills become more effective and automatic.

The modular nature of the *Guide* means that users need not follow the modules in the order presented. Your interests, strengths, and prior experience as a designer will inevitably dictate how you use this *Guide* and the sequence you follow. Think of the *Design Guide*, then, as a cookbook. In a cookbook there are chapters devoted first to recipes of appetizers, then to soups and salads, then to fish and meat, vegetables, and desserts. Similarly, the *Guide* is organized by the "menu" of a unit's parts—the elements of the unit template. But although the cookbook is organized, you need not read it from cover to cover or make all the recipes in the order in which they appear. So, too, in unit design. Like the recipe creator, your path is informed by the need to put the final work in recipe form, but recipe creation is inherently nonlinear and messy as you try things out, alter various ingredients, and double-back to ensure that the final product works.

Module I

....

Unpacking Standards

....

Purpose: To prioritize and focus on our content obligations appropriately.

Desired Results:

Unit designers will understand that

- Standards by themselves are not a curriculum; a curriculum works with the standards to frame optimal learning experiences.
- Standards and most goal statements need to be analyzed or unpacked because they may
  - be ambiguous;
  - be too broad or too narrow; and/or
  - reflect different kinds of goals simultaneously (e.g., knowledge, skill, understanding, performance indicators).
- Unpacking standards helps to clarify the long-term intentions behind the standards, distinguish among goal types, and focus unit planning.

Unit designers will be able to

- Unpack standards and other established goals that apply to the unit, and place them in the proper Stage 1 boxes.

Module Design Goals: In this Module, you will learn various ways to unpack standards and other goals to properly identify the various Stage 1 elements. The end product will be a refined set of desired results identified in Stage 1.

You should work on Module I if you are obligated to pre-established standards (state/provincial/national) or other goals (e.g., from a school or district mission) and if you are unfamiliar with the process of unpacking standards or other goals into the UbD Template.

You might skim or skip Module I if you are not obligated to use established local, state, or national standards or other formal goals.

....

Many users of this *Guide* will need to address externally mandated goals of some kind—most commonly state, provincial, or national standards. The UbD Template has a specific box for such established goals, on the left side of Stage 1 (see Figure I.1). This placement is meant to signal an important idea about state standards and other such obligations. The standards are *not* the primary goals of your unit design. Meeting them is necessary but not sufficient.

Consider an analogy with home building and renovation. The standards are like the building code. Architects and builders must attend to them but they are *not* the purpose of the design. The house to be built or renovated is to meet the needs of the client in a functional and pleasing manner—while also meeting the building code as a part of the larger integrated and coherent whole.

Similarly, although unit designs have to validly address external standards, we always want to keep the long-term educational ends in mind: an engaging and meaningful learning experience that develops learner understanding and curiosity while also meeting standards. That's why we place standards on the side of Stage 1. In other words, standards by themselves are not a curriculum. A curriculum works with the standards in a way to frame optimal learning experiences. The standards are more like the ingredients list for a recipe than the final meal; they are more like the rules of the game instead of strategy for succeeding at the game. A curriculum fleshes out the best ways to honor one's obligations while making learning as engaging and effective as possible.

Unpacking Standards

Standards can be somewhat opaque, and they often vary in clarity, complexity, and specificity. Some standards are broad, cutting across many courses and grade levels; others are narrow and content-specific. Some refer to content that must be taught; other standards refer to performance levels that must be achieved.

A standard has to be treated like any other nonfiction text; that is, we have to carefully analyze and interpret its meaning. A standard poses a challenge similar to the one posed by determining the meaning of the Bill of Rights in specific situations. In fact, a standard represents key principles that demand constant thought and discussion. That's what we mean by saying that educators need to "unpack" standards for local use. The practical meaning of a standard is not self-evident even if the writing is clear.

Consider this example:

Virginia History 5.7

The student will understand the causes and effects of the Civil War with emphasis on slavery, states' rights, leadership, settlement of the west, secession, and military events. [*Source:* VA Curriculum Framework United States History to 1865; Commonwealth of Virginia Board of Education Richmond, Virginia Approved—July 17, 2008]

Figure I.1

Unpacking Standards Stage 1—Mathematics

Stage 1—Desired Results		
Transfer		
Students will be able to independently use their learning to . . . Solve nonroutine problems by persevering: simplify them, interpret expressions, and use equivalent forms based on the properties of real numbers and the order of operations.		
Meaning		
UNDERSTANDINGS *Students will understand that . . .* 1. In mathematics, we accept certain truths as necessary to permit us to solve problems with logical certainty (e.g., the properties of real numbers), whereas other rules are conventions that we assume just for effective communication. 2. We can use the commutative, associative, and distributive properties to turn complex and unfamiliar expressions into simpler and familiar ones when problem solving.	**ESSENTIAL QUESTIONS** *Students will keep considering . . .* 1. What important rules and conventions are required to make algebra "work"? 2. How can we simplify this expression?	
Acquisition of Knowledge & Skill		
Established Goals **Common Core State Standards in Math** **Interpret the structure of expressions** 1. Interpret expressions that represent a quantity in terms of its context. **Write expressions in equivalent forms to solve problems** 3. Choose and produce an equivalent form of an expression to reveal and explain properties of the quantity represented by the expression. **Rewrite rational expressions** 6. Rewrite simple rational expressions in different forms. **Mathematical Practices** 1. Make sense of problems and persevere in solving them. 2. Reason abstractly and quantitatively. 3. Construct viable arguments and critique the reasoning of others.	*Students will know . . .* 1. The commutative property and to which operation it applies (and when it does not apply). 2. The associative property and to which operation it applies (and when it does not apply). 3. The distributive property and to which operation it applies (and when it does not apply). 4. The "order of operations" mathematicians use and why is it needed. 5. What PEMDAS mean. 6. What it means to "simplify" an expression via equivalent forms.	*Students will be skilled at . . .* 1. Writing expressions in equivalent forms. 2. Revealing and explaining properties represented. 3. Rewriting rational expressions in different forms. 4. Identifying equivalence that results from properties and equivalence that is the result of computation. 5. Justifying steps in a simplification or computation by citing applicable laws, properties, conventions.

Source: Goals from high school algebra standards, pp. 63–65. © Copyright 2011, National Governors Association Center for Best Practices and Council of Chief State School Officers. All rights reserved.

What does "understand" mean here? Does it mean *make meaning* of and *transfer*? Or does it mean something narrower like *analyze*? Or is the demand far more modest, namely "Accurately state and explain what others—credible experts—have analyzed the causes and effects to be, as found in textbooks" (in other words "understand" = "know")? As you can see, how we teach and how we assess this standard is greatly affected by the outcome of our inquiry. Such unpacking is essential at the local level if the standards are to be validly and consistently addressed across teachers, given the ambiguity of the key verb.

Even if we agree on what "understand" means here, there is a second question that must still be considered: What is an adequate understanding for a 5th grader? In other words, how well must a student understand the causes and effects? How sophisticated should that understanding be, to be a fair expectation of a 5th grader? In other words, merely knowing the content to be addressed is not enough information for local action. We need to analyze all relevant text to infer a reasonable performance standard for assessing student work, that is, to know when student work related to the standard is or isn't meeting the standard.

Structure and Organization of Standards

Another reason for unpacking has to do with the fact that standards are typically written in a hierarchical outline form. In many documents, the first level is the most broad and comprehensive statement, and the second and third levels are typically more concrete and narrowly focused. Each discrete element and outcome of learning is listed in an analytic fashion.

Alas, as we well know from experience what seems like a good idea in theory—a hierarchical list of key elements—has an unfortunate common unintended consequence. Some educators think that standards, arranged as organized in lists, need to be covered, one by one, in lessons and units. Not only is this practice unwise pedagogically; it is not the writers' intent. Some standards documents offer explicit cautions against such decontextualized teaching; for example:

> Many of the objectives/benchmarks are interrelated rather than sequential, which means that **objectives/benchmarks are not intended to be taught in the specific order in which they are presented. Multiple objectives/benchmarks can and should be taught at the same time.** [emphasis in the original]
>
> *Source*: 2007 Mathematics Framework, Mississippi Department of Education, p. 8

Here is how the Common Core State Standards in English Language Arts are introduced:

> While the Standards delineate specific expectations in reading, writing, speaking, listening, and language, each standard need not be a separate

focus for instruction and assessment. Often, several standards can be addressed by a single rich task. (*Source:* Common Core State Standards for English Language Arts and Literacy in History/Social Studies, Science, and Technical Subjects, p. 5)

Alas, this advice is routinely overlooked or ignored in local curriculum work. And yet the distinction between discrete elements and a more integrated curriculum plan is just common sense. A good meal is more than just the listed ingredients in the recipe; a successful home renovation doesn't merely involve contractors addressing each isolated piece of the building code; music is not made by learning hundreds of discrete notes, key signatures, and tempos in isolation from performance. In fact, if transfer and meaning making are the goals of education, they can *never* be achieved by a curriculum that just marches through discrete content elements, no matter how sensible the hierarchical list is as an *outline* of a subject's high points.

Misconception Alert

Standards documents are written in a hierarchical list format. This analytic framing of standards can easily mislead teachers into the following misconceptions:

- The standard clearly expects me to teach and test each objective in isolation.
- I'll just focus on the top level (i.e., the broadest) standard. Then, I can justify most of what I already do as meeting the standard.
- I'll just focus on the lowest levels and check off these very specific objectives that are covered in my normal unit. Then, I have addressed the standard.

Each claim is inaccurate and leads to needlessly isolated and ineffective teaching and assessment.

Different Goal Types in the Standards

A third reason for unpacking standards results from the fact that standards not only come in different shapes and sizes, but typically address different *types* of learning goals. It is not uncommon for a standard to mix together acquisition, meaning, and transfer goals in the same list without calling attention to the fact that each type of goal is different and likely requires different instructional and assessment treatments. Here is an example from the Common Core State Standards for 5th grade math:

Number and Operations in Base Ten—5.NBT

Understand the place value system.

1. Recognize that in a multi-digit number, a digit in one place represents 10 times as much as it represents in the place to its right and 1/10 of what it represents in the place to its left.

2. Explain patterns in the number of zeros of the product when multiplying a number by powers of 10, and explain patterns in the placement of the decimal point when a decimal is multiplied or divided by a power of 10. Use whole-number exponents to denote powers of 10.
3. Read, write, and compare decimals to thousandths.
4. Use place value understanding to round decimals to any place.

As we interpret the standards, 1 and 2 are really about meaning-making (though the verb "recognize" may lull some into thinking that this is about low-level acquisition), 3 is a mixture of acquisition ("read and write") and meaning-making ("compare"), and 4 could be either skill focused or transfer focused, depending upon how novel, complex, and unprompted the tasks given to students. The careful interpretation is why it is neither redundant to have a separate section on the Template for unit-relevant standards (or established long-term goals) nor superfluous to place the appropriate parts of a standard into the Stage 1 and 2 boxes, with additional clarifying language when needed. *When completed, Stage 1 provides evidence that the standards were unpacked in a transparent way, and shows how the various goals properly relate to one another.*

So, rather than simply lumping all standards together and calling them your unit goals, we strongly recommend that designers carefully examine each standard and place its components—whether stated or implied—in the *appropriate* Stage 1 box: Transfer, Essential Questions, Understandings, Knowledge, or Skill.

Misconception Alert

Be careful if you work in a state that makes reference to "big ideas" and "essential questions" in their standards. They do not always correspond to how we define these terms in UbD. For example, Florida highlights certain standards by labeling them big ideas, but this use of the phrase is meant to simply signal *priorities* in general rather than specific transferable ideas to be grasped and used.

MA.5.A.2, BIG IDEA 2: Develop an understanding of and fluency with addition and subtraction of fractions and decimals. (*Source:* www.floridastandards.org/Standards/PublicPreviewIdea196.aspx)

Similarly, some states have listed essential questions in their standards or resource documents, but most of these would not meet the UbD design standard. For example, consider two listed "essential questions" in *The Virginia History and Social Science Standards of Learning Curriculum Framework 2008*, a companion document to the 2008 *History and Social Science Standards of Learning:*

- What are the seven continents?
- What are the five oceans?

Although these questions may point toward important knowledge, they are certainly *not* essential in the UbD sense because they are factual questions, not designed to cause in-depth inquiry and discussion. In sum, beware—especially when familiar jargon is used in the documents.

Turning Standards into Sound Curriculum, Instruction, and Assessment

Based on these cautions and mindful of the need for practical tools in working through these issues, we offer the following five tips for unpacking the standards.

Tip 1. Look at all key verbs to clarify and highlight valid student performance in which content is used. Carefully analyze the verbs and try to determine their meaning for assessment and thus instruction. For example, does "respond to" mean "resonate with" or "write about" or "make a personal connection to the text"? What counts as "understanding" the causes and effects of the Civil War? For example, does "understand" in this case mean "accurately recall what the textbook said" were the major causes? Or are the students expected to make their own analyses, based on primary and secondary source evidence, and also defend them? Obviously, the answers affect the overall unit design and, especially, the assessments.

One would hope, of course, that the language used in standards documents is consistent and grounded in a valid framework such as Bloom's taxonomy. For example, it seems reasonable to assume that phrases like "analyze" or "solve problems" are meant to signal more higher-order inferential work than is required by standards that say "describe" or "identify."

Our experience from working with standards-writing committees proves that verbs are not always used in a consistent or appropriate manner. Nor are glossaries containing operational definitions of key verbs usually provided. Making matters worse, most standards documents do not state whether there is a *pedagogical* rationale behind the use of specific verbs or instead whether the verbs vary for *aesthetic* reasons (to avoid repetition in the text).

We recommend that your committee members scour relevant websites and communicate with state education departments to clarify this basic issue when necessary. We also highly recommend that educators look at whatever test specifications exist for state standards because the test-maker needs this same information in order to construct valid measures. In some states, the test specifications found under the state assessment section are more helpful than the standards themselves. For example, take a look at Florida Math Test Specifications at http://fcat.fldoe.org/pdf/G9-10_Math_Specs_1-39.pdf.

Tip 2: Look at the recurring nouns that signal big ideas. A related approach to unpacking standards involves finding important nouns, that is, key concepts, principles, themes, and issues that can be turned into essential questions and understandings. Here is an example from the Common Core State Standards that illustrate this approach (bold added to key nouns that signify big ideas):

Expressions and Equations 7.EE

Use **properties of operations** to generate **equivalent expressions**.

1. Apply properties of operations as strategies to add, subtract, factor, and expand linear expressions with rational coefficients.
2. Understand that rewriting an expression in different forms in a problem context can shed light on the problem and how the quantities in it are related. *For example, a + 0.05a = 1.05a means that "increase by 5%" is the same as "multiply by 1.05."* (p. 49)

Notice how the phrases we boldface also suggest possible essential questions and Understandings that could be put in the UbD planner:

- How can we simplify this problem by using equivalent expressions and properties? How can we rewrite this equation to reveal important relationships and meanings?
- Problem solving often requires finding equivalent expressions in which complex elements are made simpler and more familiar via the properties of operations.

Tip 3: Identify and analyze the key adjectives and adverbs to determine valid scoring criteria and rubrics related to successful performance against the standards. The qualifiers of the verbs and nouns can provide a useful and efficient way to build a set of local rubrics to ensure that assessment is standards based and consistent across assignments. Here is an example, using a reading standard, in which key qualifiers are in bold and implicit qualifiers are added in italics:

Cite **strong and thorough** textual evidence to support *an accurate and justified* analysis of what the text says explicitly as well as inferences drawn from the text, including determining where the text leaves matters uncertain. (From Common Core State Standards ELA, Grades 11–12. Key Ideas and Details, Informational Text p. 40)

So the rubric titles might be Quality of Evidence Cited and Quality of Analysis Made.

Tip 4. Identify and/or infer the long-term transfer goals by looking closely at the highest-level standards and indicators for them, or inferring the transfer goal from the content and justification for the standard. Even if the standard stresses important content, it typically states or implies key performance related to that content. In other words, if that's the content, what are students eventually expected to do with it? Long-term transfer goals answer the "Why are we learning this?" question. Ask yourself

- What should students be able to do well on their own while using this content, to truly meet this standard and its purpose? (*complex performance ability*)

- What does "perform well" mean for each standard? (*specific performance standards and criteria for evaluating complex performance*)

In the event that the documents for your state, province, or nation do not identify such long-term performance goals, we recommend that you look at the introductory pages for each discipline. Larger goals, purposes, or intentions of the standards are often presented in the opening section before the specifics are listed.

Tip 5: Consider the standards in terms of the long-term goal of autonomous performance. To stress the transfer aspect of the goal, make a point of highlighting the idea that students are expected to perform with content autonomously. The most concrete and helpful way to do this is to make explicit and write in a phrase that is unfortunately implicit in most standards: ***on their own***. Students must be able to use content autonomously, without the need for extensive scaffolding, reminders, and hints. So, add "on their own" to each standard to better grasp the kind of independent transfer expected.

Now, consider how the use of this phrase could influence assessment and instruction. For example, it suggests the need for a "gradual release" of teacher direction over time so that learners develop increasing capacity for independent performance. The following examples, from the Common Core State Standards, in which we added the key phrase, underscore this point:

GRADE 5 READING: Key ideas and details.

*Students **on their own***

1. Quote accurately from a text when explaining what the text says explicitly and when drawing inferences from the text.
2. Determine two or more main ideas of a text and explain how they are supported by key details; summarize the text.
3. Explain the relationships or interactions between two or more individuals, events, ideas, or concepts in a historical, scientific, or technical text based on specific information in the text. (*Source:* Common Core State Standards, p. 12)

GRADE 8 MATHEMATICS: Functions.

*Students **on their own***

- Define, evaluate, and compare functions.
- Use functions to model relationships between quantities.
(*Source:* Common Core State Standards, p. 53)

Far too many teachers heavily scaffold learning activities, discussions, exercises, and assessments right up until the end of the year. Students then get too little practice and feedback in identifying main ideas or solving multistep problems *on their own*. It should not surprise us, then, when students do poorly on these abilities on standardized tests.

In fact, the Common Core State Standards document in English Language Arts explicitly stresses independence as one of seven key traits that present an emerging "portrait of students who meet the standards":

They demonstrate independence.

Students can, without significant scaffolding, comprehend and evaluate complex texts across a range of types and disciplines, and they can construct effective arguments and convey intricate or multifaceted information. Likewise, students are able independently to discern a speaker's key points, request clarification, and ask relevant questions. They build on others' ideas, articulate their own ideas, and confirm they have been understood. Without prompting, they demonstrate command of standard English and acquire and use a wide-ranging vocabulary. More broadly, they become self-directed learners, effectively seeking out and using resources to assist them, including teachers, peers, and print and digital reference materials. (p. 7)

Using other Common Core Standards, we offer additional examples about how the standards can be unpacked to represent every element in Stage 1 of the Template in Figures I.2 and I.3.

Figure I.4 is worksheet designed as a matrix to help you unpack standards.

Design Tip: Here are some basic rules for interpreting established standards:

- Look closely at verbs, but be aware that not all standards documents use verbs consistently to signal the type of goal or degree of cognitive demand. Check your state or provincial documents for guidance.
- Some standards statements begin with a low-level verb (identify, describe, state). Don't be confused into thinking that this automatically signals a skill. Generally, such statements call for knowledge. For example, "Identify parts of speech" specifies declarative knowledge because it means that "the student will know the parts of speech," despite the action verb in the beginning. Look at the test specifications for the standards for clarification.
- When higher-order verbs are used (analyze, infer, generalize), the goal can be ambiguous. If the verb is followed by or describes general abilities, it is likely stating a transfer goal. However, the verb may be used as a performance indicator and thus will be more useful for determining specific assessment evidence in Stage 2. (See the following section for further discussion.)

Online you will find worksheets set up in different ways and with varying examples to help you unpack standards. Figure I.5, Unpacking Standards Worksheet—Reading; Figure I.6, Unpacking Standards Worksheet—English Language Arts; Figure I.7, Unpacking Standards Matrix—Mathematics; Figure I.8, Unpacking Standards Matrix—History; Figure I.9, Unpacking Standards Worksheet—Civics; Figure I.10, Unpacking Standards Worksheet—Social Studies; Figure I.11, Unpacking Standards Worksheet Stages 1–3; Figure I.12, Designing Units Based on Content Standards; Figure I.13, Unpacking Standards Worksheet.

Figure I.2

Unpacking Standards Stages 1–3—English Language Arts

Key Ideas and Details ────►	Stage 1: Different Goal Types
1. Read closely to determine what the text says explicitly and to make logical inferences from it; cite specific textual evidence when writing or speaking to support conclusions drawn from the text.	What are the key higher-order VERBS, and what do they suggest the general long-term transfer goal is? *Students eventually need to be able, on their own, to…* • Determine what the text says explicitly and infer what the text implies, regardless of text or genre. What are the key NOUN CONCEPTS, and what do they suggest the big ideas to be mastered and used are? *Students will need to organize their thinking, knowledge, and skill around such ideas/questions as…* • Logical inferences. • Textual evidence. What VERBS state or imply specific skills to be mastered? *Students need to be able to demonstrate such skills as…* • Cite specific textual evidence. What key FACTS must be known and used? *Students need to know such facts as…* • Definitions of "logical," "inference," "evidence," "support." • The facts stated in the text.
──────────────►	**Stage 2: Assessment** What are the key VERBS, and what do they suggest the specific assessments need to be? *Students will need to show they can…* • Determine what the text says explicitly. • Make logical inferences (from the text). • Support conclusions drawn from the text. • Cite specific textual evidence. What are the key ADJECTIVES and ADVERBS, and what do they suggest the key criteria for judging work should be? *Student performance and products will need to reveal to what extent students …* • Read *closely*. • Make *logical* inferences. • Cite *specific* textual evidence.
──────────────►	**Stage 3: Learning Plan** What do the verbs, nouns, and verb modifiers imply for instruction? *The standard can only be reached if students are given instruction, practice, and feedback in…* • How to make sense of a text, how inference is different from inspecting the text, and seeing the difference between sound and unsound evidence and inference when claims are made about the text.

Source: Standard excerpt from College and Career Readiness Anchor Standard in *Common Core State Standards for English Language Arts and Literacy in History/Social Studies, Science, and Technical Subjects*, p. 35. © Copyright 2010. National Governors Association Center for Best Practices and Council of Chief State School Officers. All rights reserved.

Figure I.3

Unpacking Standards Worksheet—Mathematics

Common Core Best Practice #4 **Model with mathematics.** Mathematically proficient students can apply the mathematics they know to solve problems arising in everyday life, society, and the workplace. In early grades, this might be as simple as writing an addition equation to describe a situation. In middle grades, a student might apply proportional reasoning to plan a school event or analyze a problem in the community.... Mathematically proficient students who can apply what they know are comfortable making assumptions and approximations to simplify a complicated situation, realizing that these may need revision later. They are able to identify important quantities in a practical situation and map their relationships.... They can analyze those relationships mathematically to draw conclusions. They routinely interpret their mathematical results in the context of the situation and reflect on whether the results make sense, possibly improving the model if it has not served its purpose.	Transfer goals in the VERBS:	• Apply what they know to everyday problems. • Make assumptions and approximations. • Analyze relationships mathematically and draw conclusions. • Interpret results in context. • Simplify a complicated situation. • Reflect and improve model. • Be able to identify important quantities in a practical situation.
	Criteria in the ADVERBS and ADJECTIVES:	• Mathematically proficient • Context-sensitive • Comfortable • Important quantities • Routinely interpret
	Possible task ideas:	• Plan a school event. • Analyze a problem in the community.
	Stated or implied big ideas in the NOUNS:	• Simplification of a complicated situation • Proportional reasoning • Problems
	Possible Understandings: *Students will understand that...* • Mathematical models simplify and connect phenomena so that we might better understand them. • Mathematical models must be viewed critically so that they do not mislead us into thinking that reality is that simple.	Possible Essential Questions: • How can I simplify this complexity without distorting it? • How do I know if my model is a good one here (for this particular situation)? • What are the limits of my model?

Source: Standard excerpt from Common Core State Standards, Standards for Mathematical Practice, p. 7. © Copyright 2011, National Governors Association Center for Best Practices and Council of Chief State School Officers. All rights reserved.

Figure I.4

Unpacking Standards Matrix—Mathematics

Insert (within 1 or more cells) important learning activities and performance tasks that require strategic thought and real-world competence in the use of content. Refer back to the transfer and meaning goals to determine the kinds of complex work and thinking expected of students.

Math Content Standards 3rd Grade	**1** Make sense of problems and persevere in solving them	**2** Reason abstractly and quantitatively	**3** Construct viable arguments and critique the reasoning of others	**4** Model with mathematics	**5** Use appropriate tools strategically	**6** Attend to precision	**7** Look for and make use of structure	**8** Look for and express regularity in repeated reasoning
Represent and solve problems involving multiplication and division.	*5–6 authentic performance tasks of increasing complexity over the course of the year in which students have to figure out what the problem is asking, figure out which operation to use and when to use it, develop a general math model for such problems, and defend an answer in a realistic situation. For example: prepare a budget for a class trip, a home renovation, a year's wardrobe, mindful of budget constraints and unit costs, etc.*							
Understand properties of multiplication and the relationship between multiplication and division.								
Multiply and divide within 100.								
Solve problems involving the four operations, and identify and explain patterns in arithmetic.								
Use place value understanding and properties of operations to perform multidigit arithmetic.								
Develop understanding of fractions as numbers.	*3–4 authentic tasks requiring students ON THEIR OWN to realize that fractions are involved, determine the fractions, and use operations on the fractions to calculate solutions, and represent their findings graphically.*							
Solve problems involving measurement and estimation of intervals of time, liquid volumes, and masses of objects.						*Activities and assessments that require students to judge, calculate, and defend the appropriate degree of precision in varied contexts where precision needs vary.*		
Represent and interpret data.								
Geometric measurement: understand concepts of area and relate area to multiplication and to addition.								

Source: Excerpt from mathematical practices and grade 3 overview standards, p. 22. © Copyright 2010, National Governors Association Center for Best Practices and Council of Chief State School Officers. All rights reserved.

Addressing the Standards

A clear understanding of standards is necessary but insufficient because we need to know what follows for instruction and, especially, assessment. Unless our local assessments properly assess against the standards, as noted earlier, we will unwittingly only refer to the standards instead of actually meeting them. Thus, a key design question is as follows: how much assessment evidence and instruction, and of what kind, is needed to fully *address* and *meet* the standards?

By definition, in UbD any goal (including a standard) is only "addressed" if we address it *explicitly* in Stage 2 and Stage 3. Yet, we have observed a tendency for some designers to list every conceivably relevant standard in Stage 1 that *may* come into play, no matter how superficially. Too often, designers simply check off that the unit *relates* to a standard without actually teaching and assessing it. For example, in a high school unit on persuasive writing, the temptation is to list benchmarks related to rules of grammar or subject-verb agreement—and then, for good measure, reference all the speaking and listening standards because they will be discussed. While such skills are certainly related to the unit topic, they are *not* the main focus of this unit; and assessments only touch on them incidentally. We discourage listing all facts, concepts, or skills that *might* be used within the unit.

Our rule of thumb is straightforward: only list the standards that are explicitly assessed and taught to. Otherwise, you will deceive yourselves about how well the standards have been addressed and be even more prone to "teaching by mentioning"—that is, listing the standard on a unit plan or posting it on the board without any in-depth instruction or assessment. Such practices do *not* constitute a standards-based system. A standard is only addressed if the unit *validly assesses* for its achievement (Stage 2) and if there are *multiple relevant learning opportunities* to help students achieve it (Stage 3). In addition, most standards would only be fully addressed once the standard is addressed in multiple units.

⟳ **Design Tip:** A standard or benchmark should only be listed in Stage 1 if it is explicitly assessed in Stage 2 and included in one or more learning events in Stage 3. Furthermore, when sharing units with other teachers, indicate whether the listed standard should receive minor emphasis and be addressed in a few learning events, or major emphasis and be addressed in numerous learning events and assessed.

Local Assessment: Where the Rubber Meets the Road

"Addressing" the standards in teaching and assessment design is necessary but not sufficient. The aim is for student performance to meet the standards or exceed them. After all, standards aren't met by what the teacher designs and does, but are met through the work that students produce. Thus the question when we consider standards implementation: *Is student work up to standard* (even if the assessments we designed validly address the standards)? If we have truly addressed the standards (as reflected in valid assessments) and if students have truly met the standards locally (as reflected in valid and reliable scoring), then we should be confident about their ability to perform on tests designed backward from the same standards.

Alas, the inability to make such an accurate prediction is arguably one of the greatest weaknesses in U.S. education: local tests and grades rarely predict state and national performance, with dire consequences for students, teachers, and administrators. By contrast, think of sports where we can see in weekly results (based on time) how our team stacks up against local, regional, state, and national competition. A coach at a small school does not deceive herself about student performance. The official times tell a different tale: not one of her runners is likely to place in the top 50 in the end-of-season regional or sectional meet. The sooner the runners know this, the better. And the same is true for academic achievement.

That is why more and more schools have signed on to provide Advanced Placement or International Baccalaureate classes. Our point is not to promote these or any other programs, but such adoption is sensible if we want to be sure that local assessment is valid and compares reasonably with assessments used in other schools. The ideal solution, we think, is to strive for valid and rigorous local assessment, with regular audits of such validity and rigor, so that students, parents, and other stakeholders can have confidence in local assessment.

Our students and their coaches, or teachers, need to know where they really stand week in and week out against established performance benchmarks. Local assessments must aspire to give us information about that standing, whether or not we adopt external programs. No surprises, no excuses. We should know where we stand against standards before it is too late to do anything about it.

Mission-Related (and Other Established) Goals

Whether you are obligated to state or national standards, there are typically other long-term established goals to consider in Stage 1. For example, the mission statement of a district or school contains outcomes that can and must be included in unit plans somewhere. Similarly, some states and districts have committed to cultivating 21st century skills, which need to be woven into unit designs. As a practical matter, in almost every state there are subjects and topics taught for which there are no externally established standards or standardized tests (e.g., physics or drawing). Presumably there are local program goals for these areas, and they should be placed in the Goals box and unpacked into the other appropriate Stage 1 boxes on the Template. While people within and outside schools acknowledge the importance of goals like critical thinking and effective teamwork, worthy goals of this sort often fall through the cracks of day-to-day teaching and assessing. Indeed, in many schools these important aims become mere platitudes or empty rhetoric on plaques in the hall rather than obligatory long-term objectives.

Self-Assessment and Peer Assessment

Use the following questions to self-assess the Stage 1 portion of your draft unit plan. Unit designers can sometimes get too close to their work, therefore we recommend that you show your plan to a colleague and ask him or her for feedback as well. See Module P for an in-depth account of self-assessment and peer review.

- Are all goals (including those derived from standards and other established goals) properly placed as transfer (T), understandings (U), knowledge (K), and skill (S)?
- Does Stage 1 include *only* those goals that will be explicitly taught and assessed?
- Is there proper alignment among the various Stage 1 goals?

Further Information on the Ideas and Issues in This Module

Understanding by Design, 2nd ed. (Wiggins & McTighe, 2005). Chapter 3, "Gaining Clarity on Our Goals," offers an extended discussion of the issues raised in this module. A review of Chapter 1 on backward design may be useful for novices to this approach to unit design. The most practical discussion of goals and what they imply is found in Chapter 11 on the design process, in which the original template is described and a typical unit is shown before (without using) understanding by design, and how that unit is transformed by using UbD.

Understanding by Design: Professional Development Workbook (McTighe & Wiggins, 2004). Examples, worksheets and design tools for unpacking standards to identify understandings and essential questions derived from standards can be found on pages 81–83, 104–105, and 120–125.

Schooling by Design: Mission, Action, and Achievement (Wiggins & McTighe, 2007). Chapter 1 discusses mission and standards to show how many state standards at the highest level focus on transfer as a goal. Chapter 2 discusses the idea of the curriculum "blueprint" and purpose as separate from "meeting the building code"—addressing content standards. Chapter 3 discusses how district/school curriculum should be developed with a focus on transfer goals and big ideas.

Module J

....

Identifying Evaluative Criteria for Assessments

....

Purpose: To identify the most appropriate evaluative criteria for assessments, mindful of the desired results from Stage 1.

Desired Results:

Unit designers will understand that

- Valid assessment requires appropriate criteria for evaluating student work. Appropriate criteria are derived primarily from the Stage 1 goals being assessed, not just from the surface features of a particular assessment task.

- Evaluative criteria should correspond to the most salient features that distinguish understanding and masterful transfer performance, not merely those qualities that are easiest to see or score.

- Complex performance involves different aspects, so unit assessments typically involve varied criteria so that students can receive the most helpful feedback.

- Rubrics are evaluative tools based on criteria. There are two widely used types of rubrics—holistic and analytic.

- Students may be given product/performance choices within an assessment task, but the evaluative criteria and rubric must remain consistent—that is, aligned with the goals of Stage 1 (and the choices must provide valid indicators of what is being measured).

Unit designers will be able to

- Develop the most appropriate criteria for use in their Stage 2 assessments. These criteria will be the basis for more detailed scoring rubrics.

Module Design Goals: In this module, you will learn to distinguish among four types of evaluative criteria and how to select and weight appropriate criteria based on Stage 1 goals.

You should work on Module J if you have not already considered or identified appropriate evaluative criteria for your assessments in Stage 2.

You might skim or skip Module J if you have already identified appropriate evaluative criteria or have appropriate scoring tools (rubrics, checklists) for your assessments, reflecting Stage 1 goals.

We have made the case (Wiggins & McTighe, 2011) for using open-ended performance assessments to gather evidence that students understand and can transfer their learning. So how should we evaluate their performance on assessments tasks and prompts that do not result in a single "correct" answer or solution process? In this module we explore how to identify and use appropriate evaluative criteria.

Benefits of Criterion-Based Evaluation

Clearly defined criteria are used to guide evaluative judgments about products and performances related to the overall goals identified in Stage 1. The clarity provided by well-defined criteria helps to make a judgment-based process as consistent and defensible as possible when evaluating student performance. Look at the example from a driver's education unit shown in Figure J.1. Regardless of the task specifics or who is doing the judging, we would look for drivers to be (1) skillful, (2) courteous, (3) defensive, (4) responsive to conditions, and (5) law-abiding. From those five criteria we can then build rubrics useful to both students and would-be judges. In fact, we can then also construct a variety of valid driving tasks to evoke those kinds of behaviors. More generally, when agreed-upon criterion-based assessment tools are used throughout a department or grade-level team, school, or district, more consistent grading and test design occur because the criteria and their weight do not vary from teacher to teacher.

A second benefit of criterion-based evaluation tools relates to teaching. Clearly defined criteria provide more than just evaluation tools to use at the end of instruction; they help make performance goals transparent for all. For instance, specifying indicators and examples of what defensive driving looks like (and what other driving looks like) becomes part of the instructional plan so that the learners can use these indicators when watching others drive and when practicing on their own.

Practice in using criteria and indicators helps teachers as well as students. Educators who have scored student work as part of a large-scale performance assessment at the district, state, or national level often observe that the process of evaluating student work against established criteria teaches them a great deal about what makes the products and performances successful. As teachers internalize the qualities of solid performance, they become more attentive to those qualities in their teaching and provide more specific and helpful feedback to learners.

Figure J.1

Evaluative Criteria and Related Evidence for Driver's Education Unit

Evaluative Criteria	Assessment Evidence
Performance is judged in terms of—	*Students will show their learning by . . . .*
	TRANSFER TASK(S):
• Skillful	1. Drive from home to school and back, with parental and teacher supervision. The goal is to demonstrate skillful, responsive, and defensive driving under real-world conditions.
• Courteous	
• Defensive	2. Same task as 1 but with rainy conditions.
• Responsive to conditions	
• Law-abiding	3. Same task as 1 but in rush-hour traffic.
	OTHER EVIDENCE:
• Accurate	4. Student self-assessment of driving and parking in Tasks 1–3 in terms of courteous and defensive behavior. Discuss adjustments made.
• Perceptive	
• Skilled	5. Observation of student driver in a driving simulator or car off road.
• Knowledgeable	6. Written test required for getting a license.
• Proficient	7. Road test required for getting a license.

Similar benefits apply to students. When students know the criteria *in advance* of their performance, they have clear, stable goals for their work (especially when they also see complementary samples of work that make the criteria concrete). There is then no mystery as to the desired elements of quality or the basis for evaluating (and grading) products and performances. Students don't have to guess about what is most important or how their work will be judged.

In addition, by sharing the criteria and related evaluation tools with students, we offer them the opportunity to self-assess as they work—a key element in student achievement gains. Using criterion-based evaluation tools as a part of instruction helps students to get their minds around important elements of quality and to use that knowledge to improve their performance along the way. Thus the criteria serve to *enhance* the quality of student learning and performance, not simply to evaluate it.

Criteria Derived from Stage 1

Consideration of criteria brings us to an important understanding for unit designers about the connection between Stages 1 and 2. The most appropriate criteria are derived from the Stage 1 goals being assessed, *not* primarily from a particular assessment task. This may seem odd at first. Aren't evaluative criteria determined *after* you have identified the assessment task? No! Consider an essay. Regardless of the specifics of any essay prompt, we should judge *all* essays against the same criteria—the qualities that make an essay effective. Thus criteria tell us where to look and what to look for in *specific* task performance to determine the extent to which the more *general* goals have been achieved.

This insight is signaled in the UbD Template by the location of the Criteria column to the left of the Performance Task section. This placement is meant to suggest that the criteria need to be considered first based on the desired results of Stage 1. Note that this idea is exemplified in the driver's education example—the same four criteria are used to assess the second and third performance tasks because they are derived from the overall goals of "skillful" and "responsive" driving.

In sum, the logic of backward design is common sense. The unit goals of Stage 1 dictate the needed assessments *as well as* the associated criteria and their weights.

Design Tip: Because good feedback is specific, you may want to add concrete indicators related to the unique aspects of the task. For example, the general trait of "defensive driving" may look different in varied driving tasks. Therefore, we might frame our rubrics with the general trait first, followed by task-specific indicators, as follows:

DEFENSIVE DRIVING: Students indicate that they drive defensively in this particular situation by _____.

Thus the key criteria are prominent and recurring, whereas the feedback is concrete and specific for each situation.

The Need for Multiple Criteria

Because most complex performances have multiple dimensions, we typically need to use multiple criteria for evaluation. For example, in a problem-solving task, a solution needs to be not only accurate but also supported by sound reasoning and evidence. Similarly, a graphic design needs to be well executed while also communicating an idea or emotion.

The need for multiple criteria does not mean to imply that "more is better." In fact, the challenge is to identify the smallest set of valid and independent criteria. Valid criteria are those that are essential to genuinely successful work, not arbitrary or merely easy to score. Independent criteria are those that are not linked to other criteria in how performance unfolds—that is, successfully meeting one criterion has little bearing on the other criteria. For example, one science lab report could have conclusions unsupported by evidence even though the lab procedures were meticulously followed, whereas another report could show sloppy record keeping yet provide an insightful and well-supported conclusion. In other words, following procedures is independent from well-supported conclusions. Or one student's essay might be mechanically correct but dull, whereas another student's essay might be riddled with errors in spelling and grammar but fascinating. *Mechanically correct* and *thought-provoking* are independent of one another.

What we have said about independent and useful criteria is evident in our driving example (Figure J.1). Recall that on-the-road performances are evaluated against five criteria: (1) skillful, (2) courteous, (3) defensive, (4) responsive to conditions, and (5) law-abiding. Notice again that one could be skilled but not law-abiding, and vice versa; one could be attentive but not defensive, and vice versa.

Thus the best scoring system uses the most feasible set of valid and independent criteria. In practice, this means that scorers usually use three to six independent criteria in judging complex work in order to optimize the balance of high-quality feedback and efficiency of scoring.

In short, our concern about the validity of the set of criteria is a variant of the two-question validity test for assessments (see Module D, Wiggins & McTighe, 2011). In this case, however, we are "testing" the validity of the criteria used to evaluate work, not the task itself, with these questions:

- Could the proposed criteria be met, but the overall performance still not achieve its purpose and reveal the understanding and proficiency targeted in Stage 1?
- Could the proposed criteria not be fully met, yet the overall performance appropriately assesses the targeted goals in Stage 1?

If the answer to either question is yes, then the criteria need rethinking. Now try the two-question test with the criteria *you* have identified for your assessments.

Different Types of Criteria

A complex performance involves not only varied criteria but also criteria of different types. "Is the graphic display informative?" is a different kind of question than "Is the graphic display attractive?" Similarly, asking "Was the solution effective?" is not the same as asking "Was the process efficient?" The first question in each case refers to the purpose and desired impact, whereas the latter question refers to the quality of the process or content.

Indeed, it is common for judges in various fields to distinguish between content and process. Figure J.2 illustrates the difference in the two types with sample indicators provided for each category.

Figure J.2

Two Types of Criteria with Related Indicators

CONTENT	PROCESS
accurate	mechanically sound
valid	original/creative
insightful	precise
appropriate	poised
comprehensive	polished
justified	well crafted

Note, however, that impact of performance (was the performance successful?) is not addressed by either process or content types of criteria, something we think is a common error in scoring student work. Thus we have found it helpful to expand the categories to identify four different kinds of criteria that may be relevant in complex and authentic performances. These four types are listed and exlained in Figure J.3.

Why would we argue for these four types of criteria, when it seems to make matters complicated? Let's consider each type of criterion and its importance.

Impact is clearly at the heart of what we seek in authentic performance tasks; that is, did the performance work? Did it achieve the desired result—irrespective of effort, attitude, methods used? Note how considering impact returns us to a fundamental question: What is the purpose of the performance? Or more generally, what's the point of the learning? Students need to be reminded that in performance, the bottom line matters. If the work was meant to be entertaining, informative, or persuasive—and it wasn't—then the performance did not achieve the desired result, no matter what other strengths are evident.

Figure J.3

Four Types of Criteria

Impact—Refers to the success or effectiveness of performance, given the purpose and audience.
Content—Refers to the appropriateness and relative sophistication of the understanding, knowledge, and skill employed.
Quality—Refers to the overall quality, craftsmanship, and rigor of the work.
Process—Refers to the quality and appropriateness of the procedures, methods, and approaches used— before and during performance.

Content refers to the degree of understanding or proficiency evident in student work. This category includes such indicators as accuracy, thoroughness, and quality of explanation. Was the final answer or work on target? Was the content correct or complete? Did the student address the question asked? Was the use of content sufficiently sophisticated? Did the performance reflect knowledge, skill, and understanding?

Quality refers to such elements as attention to detail, craftsmanship, mechanics, neatness, or creativity in the product or performance. Was the paper grammatically sound? Was the oral presentation fluent? Was the poster colorful and unique? Were the data in the table neatly recorded?

Process refers to the approach taken or the methods used in performance or in preparation for performance. Were directions followed? Was the manner fluid and poised? Was the performer dedicated and persistent? Did the learner practice and prepare fully? Were the students on task in their group? Did they collaborate well? These are process-related questions.

Note that these four types are fairly independent of one another. The content may be excellent, but the process could be inefficient and ineffective; the content and process might have been appropriate, but the work quality could still be shoddy. Most important, the content, process, and work quality could be fine, but the desired impact might still not have been achieved—in that situation, with that audience, given that purpose.

Here is an example in which all four types of criteria are used to evaluate a meal in nine different ways:

Goal: With a partner, cook a healthy and tasty meal for a specific group of people with varied dietary needs and interests.

Impact

1. Meal is nutritious.
2. Meal is pleasing to all guests.

Content

3. Meal reflects knowledge of food, cooking, and diners' needs and tastes.

4. Meal contains appropriate, fresh ingredients.

5. Meal reflects sophisticated flavors and pairings.

Quality

6. Meal is presented in an aesthetically appealing manner.

7. All dishes are cooked to taste.

Process

8. Meal is efficiently prepared, using appropriate techniques.

9. The two cooks collaborated effectively.

Note that these nine criteria are appropriate and independent: a meal could meet criteria 1, 3, 4, 6, 8, and 9 but not meet criteria 2, 5, 7.

However, in reality, nine criteria are too many to manage, so we could collapse the nine criteria to three without sacrificing too much in the way of feedback: Meal is *nutritious*, *pleasing*, and *well prepared*. Designers will always have to tinker with the right blend of criteria to balance the validity of the criteria, the helpfulness of the feedback, and the efficiency of the assessment.

It is important to note that although these four categories (impact, content, quality, and process) reflect common types of criteria, we do not mean to suggest that you must use all four types for every performance task. Rather, you should select the criterion types that are most appropriate for the goals being assessed through the task and for which you want to provide feedback to learners. The chart in Figure J.4 can be useful in considering which criteria to use in specific performance tasks and to ensure that each *type* of criterion is considered (more detailed rubrics can then be constructed).

⮑ **Design Tip:** Look at your draft criteria. Do they overlook or downplay the issue of impact—of the *purpose* of the performance? Do they tend to address only content, process, and work quality? Use this stem to test your criteria set: *Could the criteria I am proposing all be met but the performance/product fail to meet the purpose, the goal?*

⮑ **Design Task:** How do these four types of criteria apply to your unit's assessments? Consider which indicators reflect the most salient features, based on your targeted Stage 1 goals.

Criteria Related to Understanding

It may have occurred to you that in matters of content, the assessment decision is often simple: the content was correct or incorrect, appropriate or inappropriate. In such cases we would use a checklist to assess. However, our focus is on designing, teaching, and assessing for understanding—and understandings are rarely simply right or wrong. Unlike factual knowledge, understanding is more a matter of degree than of correctness or incorrectness. In other words, understanding is more appropriately described along a continuum, with a rubric that delineates, for example, an in-depth and sophisticated understanding, a solid understanding, an incomplete or simplistic understanding, or a misunderstanding.

Figure J.4

Four Types of Criteria with Sample Questions

Impact	Content
Was the desired result achieved?	Was the work accurate?
Was the problem solved?	Did the product reveal deep understanding?
Was the client satisfied?	Were the answers appropriately supported?
Was the audience engaged and informed?	Was the work thorough?
Was the dispute resolved?	Were the arguments of the essay cogent?
Did the speech persuade?	Was the hypothesis plausible and on target?
Did the paper open minds to new possibilities?	In sum: *Was the content appropriate to the task, accurate, and supported?*
In sum: *Was the work effective?*	
Process	**Quality**
Was the student methodical?	Was the speech organized?
Was proper procedure followed?	Was the paper mechanically sound?
Was the planning efficient and effective?	Was the chart clear and easy to follow?
Did the reader employ apt strategies?	Did the story build and flow smoothly?
Did the group work collaboratively and effectively?	Was the dance graceful?
In sum: *Was the approach sound?*	Were the graphics original?
	In sum: *Was the performance or product of high quality?*

Thus it is sometimes helpful to think through criteria related to content understanding using a set of prompting questions: *What is a sophisticated response to this issue? What is a novice response? What are some in-between responses?* The example in Figure J.5 (p. 28) shows how this might look in social studies.

 Design Tip: Given that understanding exists along a continuum, useful prompts for assessing understanding and building rubrics include these: *To what extent...? How thorough and in-depth...? How sophisticated...?*

Rubrics Based on Criteria

Our discussion thus far has focused on criteria. Although a set of criteria can be used to give feedback and evaluate performance, a more detailed rubric may be needed. A rubric is a scoring or evaluation tool that is based on identified criteria and includes a measurement scale (e.g., 4 points) and descriptions of levels of performance across the scale. Figure J.6 (p. 29) shows descriptive terms that could be used for a typical 4-point rubric.

Figure J.5

Naive to Expert Understanding: A Continuum

Use the following example to develop your own simple rubric to assess understanding of a targeted big idea or complex process along a continuum. Although you may start at any point on the continuum, it may be easiest to begin by identifying the indicators of a sophisticated, expert understanding. Then list the indicators of the understandings (and probable *mis*understandings) of a novice. Then sketch other points along the continuum. (The final rubric will require you to look at samples of work and have discussions to refine the indicators.)

Understanding the *causes and effects of the Civil War*

Naive	Knowledgeable	Expert
The naive learner	**The knowledgeable learner**	**The expert learner**
• Assumes each effect has a single cause and a single predictable effect.	• Assumes each effect can have multiple causes but that they are obvious.	• Understands that significant events typically have many causes and resulting consequences, and that some may be subtle.
• Believes that the Civil War was fought only over the morality of slavery.	• Believes that the Civil War was fought over the economics of slavery. More sophisticated: explains the cultural and economic differences between North and South.	• Recognizes that the Civil War was sparked by multiple factors, including states' rights issues, fundamental economic and cultural differences between North and South, and divided opinions about slavery.
• Concludes that the "good guys" won and the Union was preserved.	• Provides some examples of how the war's impact lasted for decades. More sophisticated: links Civil War to recent U.S. history (civil rights era, "red" and "blue" states).	• Comprehends that the war's lingering effects are evident in the form of regional loyalties and ongoing resentment of federal control.

Two general types of rubrics—holistic and analytic—are widely used to judge student performance. A holistic rubric provides an overall impression of a student's work, yielding a single rating or score. An analytic rubric divides a product or performance into distinct traits or dimensions and judges each separately. Because an analytic rubric rates each of the identified traits independently, a separate score or rating is provided for each.

So, which type of rubric should we use? Well, because these are tools, we should select the one best suited to our job. Here's a general rule of thumb: When our purpose is to provide an overall rating of a student's performance, then a holistic rubric will do. When we want more specific feedback for teachers and students, then an analytic rubric is more appropriate.

Consider the application of the two types of rubrics shown in Figure J.7. One could score the graphic displays holistically, and three students could easily end up with the same score for different reasons. Such an evaluation is by definition invalid, as well as misleading. So although holistic scoring may be easier for teachers, it often ends up sending unclear and confusing messages to students. If

Figure J.6

Descriptive Terms for Differences in Degree

Use the following general terms to describe differences in degree for constructing a scoring rubric with a 4-point scale. Once the rubric is applied, an analysis of student work will yield more precise descriptive language or a rubric with more gradations.

Degrees of Understanding
• Thorough/complete • Substantial • Partial/incomplete • Misunderstandings/serious misconceptions

Degrees of Frequency
• Always/consistently • Frequently/generally • Sometimes/occasionally • Rarely/never

Degrees of Effectiveness
• Highly effective • Generally effective • Somewhat effective • Ineffective

Degrees of Independence
Student successfully completes the task • Independently • With minimal assistance • With moderate assistance • Only with considerable assistance

Degrees of Accuracy
• Completely accurate; all _____ (facts, concepts, mechanics, computations) correct • Generally accurate; minor inaccuracies do not affect overall result • Inaccurate; numerous errors detract from result • Major inaccuracies; significant errors throughout

Degrees of Clarity
• Exceptionally clear; easy to follow • Generally clear; able to follow • Lacks clarity; difficult to follow • Unclear; impossible to follow

we applied the analytic rubric with its four different criteria (title, labels, accuracy, neatness), each student would know more precisely what was done well and what needed to be improved. Although the analytic rubric may be more time-consuming to use, the feedback is clearly more precise.

Finally, there is no need for a rubric at all if the issue is not one of degree. In that case, a simple list of things to look for will suffice. Performance lists offer a practical means of judging student performance based upon identified criteria.

A performance list consists of a set of criterion elements or traits and a rating scale. The rating scale is quite flexible, ranging from 3 to 100 points. Teachers can assign points to the various elements, in order to weight certain elements over others (e.g., accuracy counts more than neatness), based on the relative importance given the achievement target. The lists may be configured to convert easily to conventional grades. For example, a teacher could assign point values and weights that add up to 25, 50, or 100 points, enabling a straightforward conversion to a district or school grading scale (e.g., 90–100 = A, 80–89 = B) .When the lists are shared with students in advance, they provide a clear performance target, signaling to students what elements should be present in their work.

Despite these benefits, performance lists do not provided detailed descriptions of performance levels. Thus, despite identified criteria, different teachers using the same performance list may rate the same student's work quite differently.

Figure J.7

Holistic and Analytic Rubrics Compared—Examples for Graphing

Holistic Rubric

3	All data are accurately represented on the graph. All parts of the graph (units of measurement, rows, etc.) are correctly labeled. The graph contains a title that tells what the data show. The graph is very neat and easy to read.
2	Data are accurately represented on the graph *or* the graph contains minor errors. All parts of the graph are correctly labeled *or* the graph contains minor inaccuracies. The graph contains a title that tells what the data show. The graph is generally neat and readable.
1	The data are inaccurately represented, contain major errors, *or* are missing. Only some parts of the graph are correctly labeled *or* labels are missing. The title does not reflect what the data show *or* the title is missing. The graph is sloppy and difficult to read.

Analytic Rubric

Criteria:	Title	Labels	Accuracy	Neatness
Weight:	10%	20%	50%	20%
Scale 3	The graph contains a title that clearly and specifically tells what the data show. ☐	All parts of the graph (units of measurement, rows, etc.) are correctly labeled. ☐	All data are accurately represented on the graph. ☐	The graph is very neat and easy to read. ☐
2	The graph contains a title that generally tells what the data show. ☐	Some parts of the graph are inaccurately labeled. ☐	Data representation contains minor errors. ☐	The graph is generally neat and readable. ☐
1	The title does not reflect what the data show, *or* the title is missing. ☐	Only some parts of the graph are correctly labeled *or* labels are missing. ☐	The data are inaccurately represented, contain major errors, *or* are missing. ☐	The graph is sloppy and difficult to read. ☐

Assessing Independence

An additional aspect of understanding has to do with student independence or autonomy. After all, if transfer is the goal, then the assessment cannot heavily prompt and cue the learner; if it did, the ensuing performance would not show successful, independent transfer. Similarly, with meaning-making, if the teacher asks leading questions, provides lots of scaffolding graphic organizers, and reminds the learner of ideas discussed earlier, then we surely do not have adequate evidence of each student's ability to make meaning on his own.

Sometimes it is useful to have a rubric for the degree of independence shown in handling any complex assessment task, as is sometimes used in special education and vocational programs. The general rubric in Figure J.8 can be used in all performance assessments to gauge the degree of independence in a performance and to signal that the ultimate goal is student independence from teacher prompts and scaffolds. This rubric can be used as part of differentiation as well as for any ongoing formative assessment of recurring tasks or complex skills. The teacher might say, for example, that in the fall it is perfectly OK to require some teacher assistance, but by spring, on a similar task (e.g., a genre of writing or a presentation), students should strive for as little teacher assistance as possible.

Figure J.8

Rubric for Autonomous Performance (Gradual Release of Responsibility)

Level of Independence	Description
Independent	Learner completes task effectively with complete autonomy
Hints	Learning completes task with minimal assistance (e.g., 1-2 hints or guiding prompts from teacher)
Scaffolded	Learner needs step by step instructions and scaffolding (e.g., graphic organizer) to complete the task
Hand holding	Learner needs the task simplified; requires constant feedback and advice, review and reteaching; needs moral support to complete the task
Dependent	Learner cannot complete the task, even with considerable support

Design Tip: Be careful with quantitative descriptors in rubrics. We have seen many rubrics that are set up so that differences in performance levels can be "counted." For example, consider this all-too-common example of problematic scoring of a research paper: A good paper must have "more than 5 footnotes," whereas a weaker paper has "1–2 footnotes." This criterion does not pass the two-question test (refer to questions on p. 23 about the proposed criteria being met), no matter how common such criteria are in schools. We can easily imagine an insightful research paper that uses only a few resources and footnotes, but that would be viewed as a major deficiency if we focused on the number of footnotes as a criterion. Doesn't the quality of the sources matter most? Shouldn't the criterion be "well supported by appropriate sources" rather than just the number of sources? In a similar vein, teachers who give more points for the length of a paper rather than high-quality content are sending a dubious message to students about what matters in writing. Here's a rule of thumb (pun intended): Be cautious of rubrics in which you can count on your fingers to obtain a score. In other words, emphasize qualities rather than quantities in assessment.

Differentiated Assessments and Criteria

In Module N we will discuss ways of tailoring, or differentiating, your unit to address notable and constant differences in students' readiness levels, learning profiles, and interests/talents. Although differentiation is a natural approach for responsive teaching in Stage 3, we must be cautious when tailoring our assessments in Stage 2.

Consider a science standard that calls for a basic understanding of life cycles. Evidence of this understanding could be obtained by having students explain the concept and offer an illustrative example. Evidence could be collected in writing, but such a requirement would be inappropriate for an ESL student with limited skills in written English. Indeed, an ESL student's difficulty in expressing herself in writing could yield the incorrect inference that she does not understand life cycles. However, if she is offered flexibility with the response mode, such as explaining orally or visually, we will obtain a more valid measure of her understanding. In this regard, some state and district tests permit students to take math tests in their native language, to ensure that the student's knowledge of mathematics is tested fairly.

Similarly, it may well make sense to provide students with options on tests, papers, or projects whereby they can play to their strengths or preferred styles if the goal is to have a fair test that enables students to show what they know and can do; in other words, to differentiate the particulars of an assessment task.

Although we may offer product and performance options, we will almost always need to use the same evaluative criteria in judging all of the responses. This may seem counterintuitive. How could we use the same criteria if one student draws an illustrative picture and another provides a written explanation? The answer relates back to the logic of backward design and what we said earlier in this module about evaluative criteria being more general than the task: the goal in assessment is to obtain appropriate evidence of our general goals targeted in Stage 1. Assume we are looking for evidence of "understanding" and "polish" in the product. Then it doesn't matter what format or mode of communication is used. So we must be careful not to get sidetracked by the unique surface features of a product that do not directly relate to the goal.

In the previous example, we might judge every student's explanation of life cycles by the same three criteria—*accurate*, *thorough*, and inclusion of *appropriate examples*—regardless of whether a student responded orally, visually, or in writing. The criteria are derived primarily from the content goal, not the response mode. If we vary the criteria for different students, then we no longer have a valid and reliable assessment measure and our unit will be misaligned.

Of course, we want students to do high-quality work, regardless of what options they select, so we may wish to include secondary criteria related to quality. If a student prepares a poster to illustrate a balanced diet, we could look for neatness, composition, and effective use of color. Likewise, if a student made an oral presentation, we could judge pronunciation, delivery rate, and eye contact with the audience. However, it is critical to recognize that these features are linked to specific products or performances and are not the most salient criteria determined by the content goal. Here, too, we need to ensure that the relative weights of these secondary criteria are less than the primary ones related to content understanding. Figure J.9 provides a visual representation of these points.

Figure J.9

Differentiation and Uniformity Within Assessments

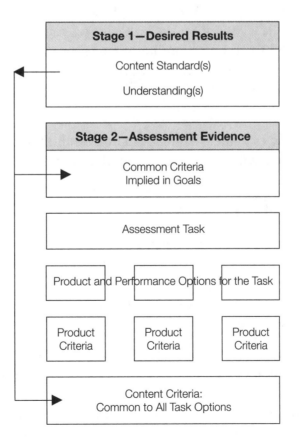

A Summary of Key Points

This has been a rich and detailed module; a summary of key points is in order. The best criteria

- Evaluate student performances in terms of characteristics central to Stage 1 goals. Be careful not to overemphasize the surface features of a particular product or performance (e.g., "colorful," "well-spoken") at the expense of the most important traits related to understanding (e.g., "thorough explanation," "accurate"). Reflect the central features of performance. Resist the temptation to focus on those elements that are easiest to see, count, or score (e.g., "at least 4 footnotes," "no misspellings") at the expense of the most important traits (e.g., "effective application," "thorough explanation").
- Split independent criteria into separate traits. In other words, do not combine distinct traits, such as "very clear" and "very organized," in the same criterion, because an essay might be clear but not organized, and vice versa.
- Emphasize the *impact* of the performance. Ultimately, meaning-making and transfer are about results. Was the paper persuasive? Was the problem solved? Was the story engaging? Was the speech informative? In other words, the criteria chosen should always highlight the purpose of a task, as indicated by results-focused criteria. Be careful not to assess for mere compliance or process (e.g., "followed all the steps," "worked hard").
- Balance specific feedback on the task with reference back to general goals. Ultimately, a broad understanding matters more than performance on a unique and very specific task. However, the indicators need to be specific enough to provide useful feedback as well as reliable scoring of the particular task.

Simply put, we should evaluate what really matters and what will provide students with the most helpful feedback long term, based on our Stage 1 goals.

Revisiting the Nutrition Unit

In earlier modules (see Wiggins & McTighe, 2011), we used a unit on nutrition to illustrate various points. Let's return to the nutrition unit to consider the evaluative criteria for the two performance tasks. In both cases, we have included the primary content criteria and the secondary quality criteria.

Task 1—Because our class has been learning about nutrition, the 2nd grade teachers in our elementary school have asked our help in teaching their students about good eating. Your task is to create an illustrated brochure to teach the 2nd graders about the importance of good nutrition for healthful living. Use cut-out pictures of food and original drawings to show the difference between a balanced diet and an unhealthy diet. Show at least two health problems that can occur as a result of poor eating. Your brochure should also contain accurate information and should be easy for 2nd graders to read and understand.

Content Criteria	**Quality Criteria**
• Accurate nutrition information provided • Clear and complete explanation of a balanced diet versus an unhealthy diet	• Neat and attractive • Two nutritionally related health problems shown

Task 2—Since we have been learning about nutrition, the camp director at the Outdoor Education Center has asked us to propose a nutritionally balanced menu for our three-day trip to the center later this year. Using the USDA guidelines and the nutrition facts on food labels, design a plan for three days, including the three main meals and three snacks (a.m., p.m., and campfire). Your goal is to create a healthy and tasty menu. In addition to your menu, prepare a letter to the director explaining how your menu meets the USDA nutritional guidelines. Include a chart showing a breakdown of the fat, protein, carbohydrates, vitamins, minerals, and calories. Finally, explain how you have tried to make your menu tasty enough for your fellow students to want to eat.

Content Criteria	**Quality Criteria**
• Menu plan that meets USDA guidelines • Clear and complete explanation of nutritional values and taste • Accurate and complete nutrition chart	• Proper letter form • Correct spelling and grammar

Design Task: What follows, then, for your own unit? Consider how can you transfer these ideas about evaluative criteria to your unit.

Self-Assessment—Review Criteria for Module J

Use the following questions to assess the evaluative criteria in your unit:

- Are the evaluative criteria directly aligned with the associated Stage 1 goals?
- Are the most appropriate evaluative criteria included for each assessment?

- Are the criteria specific enough to offer helpful feedback?
- If assessments are differentiated, are they nonetheless providing needed evidence of targeted goals?

Online you'll find the following worksheets and other helpful materials: Figure J.10, Four Types of Criteria with Descriptors/Indicators; J.11, Criterion-Based Performance List for Graphic Display of Data; Figure J.12, Naive to Expert Understanding: A Continuum Worksheet; Figure J.13, An Analytic Scoring Rubric for Understanding; Figure J.14, An Analytic Rubric Frame; Figure J.15, Holistic Rubric for Understanding; Figure J.16, Tips for Designing Effective Scoring Tools.

Further Information on the Ideas and Issues in This Module

Educative Assessment (Wiggins, 1998). Chapter 3 discusses the nature of feedback. Chapter 7 discusses rubrics and rationale and guidance on their construction and use. Chapter 10 discusses the challenge of grading and reporting when using rubrics.

Understanding by Design, 2nd ed. (Wiggins & McTighe, 2005). Chapter 8 discusses the importance and validity and how choice of scoring criteria is key.

Understanding by Design: Professional Development Workbook (McTighe & Wiggins, 2004). Stage 2. Samples of rubics and rubric worksheets can be found on pages 181–196.

Schooling by Design: Mission, Action, and Achievement (Wiggins & McTighe, 2007). Chapter 5 discusses teacher noncontact roles (what the job requires of teacher when they are not with students). Discusses the key role of teacher as developer of assessments (Role 1: Contributor to the Curriculum) and scorer of student work (Role 2: Analyzer of Results).

Scoring Rubrics in the Classroom (Arter & McTighe, 2000). A detailed book describing the characteristics, design, and use of scoring rubrics.

Guide for Instructional Leaders, Guide 2: An ASCD Action Tool (Wiggins, 2003). "Leading Curriculum Development" (pp. 1–22) discusses the link between curriculum design and assessment design.

References

McTighe, J., & Wiggins, G. (2004). *Understanding by Design: Professional development workbook*. Alexandria, VA: ASCD.

Wiggins, G. (1998). *Educative assessment: Designing assessments to inform and improve student performance*. San Francisco: Jossey-Bass.

Wiggins, G. (2003). *Guide for instructional leaders, Guide 2: An ASCD Action Tool*. Alexandria, VA: ASCD.

Wiggins, G., & McTighe, J. (2005). *Understanding by Design* (2nd ed.). Alexandria, VA: ASCD.

Wiggins, G., & McTighe, J. (2007). *Schooling by design: Mission, action, and achievement*. Alexandria, VA: ASCD.

Wiggins, G., & McTighe, J. (2011). *The Understanding by Design guide to creating high-quality units*. Alexandria, VA: ASCD.

Module K

Refining the Learning Plan in Stage 3

Purpose: To fine-tune your learning plan in Stage 3 using the first group of WHERETO elements.

Desired Results:

Unit designers will understand that

- The WHERETO elements represent qualities of effective instruction. Including them in the Stage 3 plan will result in more engaging and effective learning.

Unit designers will be able to

- Develop a learning plan that reflects the WHERETO elements and the needs of their students. (Note: The *T* for "Tailor to your students" is addressed in Module N. The *O* for "Organize the work in the best sequence" is discussed in Module O.)

Module Design Goals: In this module, you will refine your Stage 3 learning plan by incorporating ideas from the WHERE elements.

You should work on Module K (and Module J) if you wish to flesh out a more detailed and effective learning plan for Stage 3.

You might skim or skip Module K if you do not need or want a detailed learning plan at this time or if you already have well-developed learning activities and resources aligned with the unit goals.

We are now ready to complete a thorough outline of a learning plan in Stage 3. We say "outline" because this module does not require detailed lesson plans, covering every possible learning event for the entire unit.

Our goal is to ensure that the instructional plan targets the desired results identified in Stage 1 while honoring the qualities of the best learning designs.

Meeting these qualities may challenge a few habits, routines, and assumptions about instructional design and teaching "moves" for even the best teachers. Two broad criteria suggest how any learning plan and instruction should be quickly evaluated, regardless of the subject, age, experience of students, and the learning goal. Any educational experience should be *engaging* and *effective* for all learners.

By *engaging*, we mean work that is thought-provoking, meaningful, and energizing. Engaging work pulls you into the subject and makes you want to go deeper and learn more. You are intrigued by the nature of the issues, questions, mysteries, or challenges with which you are confronted. When learning is engaging, you are affected on many levels. You become emotionally and psychologically invested; you sit on the edge of your seat; you tap your toes; your pace of thought and speech pick up. If nothing else, you are so focused that time seems to pass quickly. The opposite of engaging learning is the boredom or begrudging compliance that we see when teachers simply march through dry academic content or deluge students with pointless worksheets.

By *effective*, we mean that learning is successful; that is, the desired results are achieved as fully and as efficiently as possible. Effective learning causes you to become more intellectually capable and skillful. It causes you to feel increasingly competent (instead of increasingly dumb). You develop the ability to perform to high standards, and you exceed your own and others' expectations. More to the point of your design work here, a unit is effective if the Stage 3 learning plan successfully equips students to achieve the learning goals targeted in Stage 1 and the performance tasks identified in Stage 2.

The WHERETO Elements in Instructional Planning

To ensure that the Stage 3 plan is likely to be both engaging and effective for your particular learners, we have developed the acronym WHERETO to serve as a guide. The acronym refers to important elements of instructional design and reflects best practices of pedagogy. Here is a brief introduction to the idea behind each letter:

- W—Ensure that all students understand *where* the unit is headed, and *why*.
- H—*Hook* students in the beginning and *hold* their attention throughout.
- E—*Equip* students with necessary *experiences*, tools, knowledge, and know-how to meet performance goals.
- R—Provide students with numerous opportunities to *rethink* big ideas, *reflect* on progress, and *revise* their work.
- E—Build in opportunities for students to *evaluate* progress, self-assess, and self-adjust, based on formative assessments.
- T—*Tailor* the unit to a diverse class of learners; differentiate and personalize the learning plan—without compromising Stage 1 or Stage 2.
- O—*Organize* (sequence) the unit for maximum engagement and effectiveness.

Figure K.1 provides prompting questions for each element.

Figure K.1

WHERETO Considerations for the Learning Plan

The acronym WHERETO summarizes the key elements that should be found in your learning plan, given the desired results and assessments drafted in Stages 1 and 2. Note that the elements need not appear in the same order as the letters of the acronym. Think of WHERETO as a checklist for building and evaluating the final learning plan, not a suggested sequence. For example, the learning might start with a hook (H), followed by instruction on the final performance requirements (W), then perhaps some rethinking of earlier work (R).

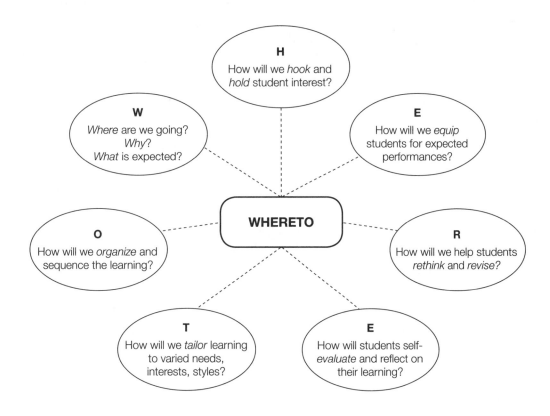

It is important to understand that WHERETO, like the six facets of understanding, serves as an analytic tool for brainstorming and a set of criteria for checking the elements of the learning plan. It does not represent a recipe or a step-by-step sequence for how to teach. As you read about each element of WHERETO, consider your own unit design. Does it adequately reflect this element? If not, what ideas come to mind? Make edits to your Stage 3 plan as needed.

Because the information related to each of these elements is extensive, we have broken up the discussion into three modules: *WHERE* (Module M), *T* (Module N), and *O* (Module O).

W—Where and Why?

Where are we headed (in terms of unit goals and priorities)? Where have we come from (in terms of connections to past learnings and checks for prior knowledge)? Why are we headed there (what is the purpose and relevance for learning this)? How will learning be assessed (what will be the key assessments and criteria/rubrics)?

Research and experience in our profession underscore common sense: learners are more likely to focus their efforts when there is a clear and worthwhile learning goal. Conversely, when the goal is unclear or irrelevant to students, it is unlikely that they will maintain attention or try their best. The *W* in *WHERE* simply reminds us as designers that we must make our unit goals clear to students. The sooner they know, in concrete performance terms, where the unit is headed, the better for all concerned. If we have done our job well in Stage 1, we should be crystal clear about the desired results in terms of understanding, knowledge, and skill. Now we want to bring that clarity to the learners.

Ideally, students will be able to answer the following questions with specificity as the unit develops:

- What will I have to understand by unit's end, and what does that understanding look like?
- What knowledge, skill, tasks, and questions must I master to demonstrate understanding and proficiency?
- What resources are available to support my learning and performance?
- What is my immediate task? How does it help me meet my long-term obligations?
- How does today's work relate to what we did previously?
- How should I allot my time? What aspects of this and future assignments demand the most attention? What has priority in the overall scheme of things?
- How will my final work be judged?

Teachers can take several practical actions in this regard, including the following:

- Directly state the desired results at the beginning of the unit, in conjunction with the overall year/course goals.
- Present the rationale for the unit/course goals.
- Identify people and places beyond the classroom where this knowledge and these skills are applied.
- Invite students to generate questions about the unit topic (the *W* in K-W-L).
- Ask students to identify personal learning goals.
- Post and discuss essential questions at the start of the unit.
- Present the culminating performance task requirements.
- Involve students in identifying appropriate evaluation criteria for the upcoming work.

- Review scoring rubrics.
- Show models and exemplars for expected products and performances.

The worksheet in Figure K.2 can help you develop learning plan elements that clarify the unit's purpose and goals for students.

Figure K.2

WHERETO Worksheet—Examples for the *W* (Where?)

Review the various ideas to help learners understand the learning goals, the purpose and relevance of the content, and what is expected of them. Also, consider how you will diagnose their prior knowledge related to the unit topic. Then check off those ideas that you will include in your learning plan.

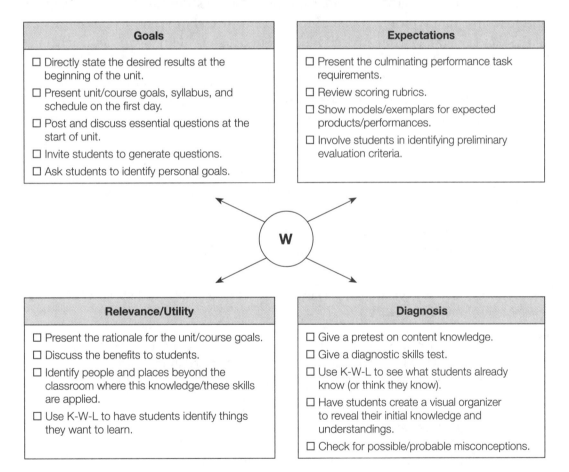

Goals	Expectations
☐ Directly state the desired results at the beginning of the unit. ☐ Present unit/course goals, syllabus, and schedule on the first day. ☐ Post and discuss essential questions at the start of unit. ☐ Invite students to generate questions. ☐ Ask students to identify personal goals.	☐ Present the culminating performance task requirements. ☐ Review scoring rubrics. ☐ Show models/exemplars for expected products/performances. ☐ Involve students in identifying preliminary evaluation criteria.

W

Relevance/Utility	Diagnosis
☐ Present the rationale for the unit/course goals. ☐ Discuss the benefits to students. ☐ Identify people and places beyond the classroom where this knowledge/these skills are applied. ☐ Use K-W-L to have students identify things they want to learn.	☐ Give a pretest on content knowledge. ☐ Give a diagnostic skills test. ☐ Use K-W-L to see what students already know (or think they know). ☐ Have students create a visual organizer to reveal their initial knowledge and understandings. ☐ Check for possible/probable misconceptions.

Design Tip: Try to design the major performance assessment tasks so that they can be distributed (along with rubrics and models) on the first or second day of the unit. This provides a clear learning/performance target for students and an instructional target for you. Designing backward from these desired performances will sharpen your goals, improve your assessments, and focus your teaching for better results.

⟳ **Design Task:** Review your present learning plan and add any ideas for helping your students better understand the units' goals, relevance, and performance expectations.

H—Hook and Hold

What thought-provoking "hooks" (e.g., experiences, problems, issues, and oddities) are likely to make the big ideas immediately interesting, tangible, and of clear importance? How might I sustain (hold) students' interest, especially when the going gets difficult?

Let us put it bluntly: schoolwork is often needlessly dull, especially when composed of skill worksheets, textbook exercises, or much passive listening. Alternatively, we know from the research as well as common sense that framing schoolwork around a provocative challenge, problem, or question can be more engaging and focusing than typical "coverage" instruction. The *H* in WHERETO reminds us of this. As a veteran teacher advised his student teacher, "Before you can teach 'em, you've got to get their attention."

Over the years, teachers have developed a variety of ways of hooking and holding students' interest in targeted topics. Here are several general approaches for introducing content to pique and sustain intellectual interest in it. Do these suggest any possible hooks suitable for your unit?

- Instant immersion in questions, problems, challenges, situations, or stories
- Thought provocations (weird facts, anomalies, discrepant events)
- Experiential shocks
- Personal and emotional connections
- Differing points of view or multiple perspectives on an issue

⟳ **Design Task:** Use the worksheet in Figure K.3 to brainstorm ideas for hooking and holding the interests of your students.

⟳ **Design Tip:** A cautionary note is in order. The goal in teaching is not merely to engage students. Be careful to ensure that the hook is purposeful and directly related to the unit's key ideas. The best hooks are both engaging and focusing.

E—Experience and Equip

What learning experiences will engage students in making meaning of the big ideas and essential questions? What learning activities, instruction, and coaching will equip students for their transfer performances?

The desired understandings identified in Stage 1 and the transfer performances specified in Stage 2 inform the nature of instruction and learning experiences needed in Stage 3. Thus backward design suggests a key meaning of the *E*: it is the teacher's job to equip the learner to make meaning and eventually perform with understanding.

Figure K.3

WHERETO Worksheet—Example for the *H* (Hook and Hold Interest)

Effective teachers recognize the importance of hooking students at the beginning of a new learning experience and holding their interest throughout. The *H* in WHERETO directs designers to consider ways of engaging students in the topic and pointing toward big ideas, essential questions, and performance tasks—by design. Use the list below to brainstorm possible hooks for your learning plan.

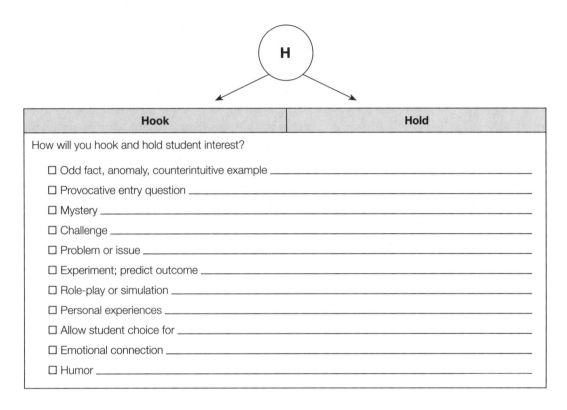

Hook	Hold
How will you hook and hold student interest?	
☐ Odd fact, anomaly, counterintuitive example _____	
☐ Provocative entry question _____	
☐ Mystery _____	
☐ Challenge _____	
☐ Problem or issue _____	
☐ Experiment; predict outcome _____	
☐ Role-play or simulation _____	
☐ Personal experiences _____	
☐ Allow student choice for _____	
☐ Emotional connection _____	
☐ Humor _____	

By using the terms *experience* and *equip*, we underscore the need for great clarity about the *meanings* we want students to make and the ultimate transfer performances we seek. In other words, our job is not to simply "cover" content. It is to help learners "uncover" (make meaning of) important ideas and effectively transfer their learning. That goal requires that we carefully consider the experiences that will help learners come to understand and equip them for autonomous transfer.

Supporting Meaning-Making

One of the ways we can equip learners to come to understand more deeply is through scaffolded instruction. Just as a builder uses a scaffold to support workers during the construction of a building, teachers can use various supports, such as graphic organizers, think-alouds, and self-assessment rubrics and guidelines, to provide a scaffold for meaning and transfer.

Consider the example in Figure K.4 in which an explicit organizer is employed to support elementary students in coming to an understanding. After introducing and modeling the organizer, the teacher facilitates the students in "adding up the facts" about pioneer life, leading to an inference. This guided approach with an organizer offers students a cognitive tool that helps them make meaning and eventually transfer the same mental process to a variety of situations in various subject areas.

Figure K.4

Making Inferences Organizer—Adding Up the Facts (Pioneer Unit)

Many pioneers, especially children, died from disease.

The pioneers had to grow or hunt for their food. Often they went hungry.

Much hard work was required to settle new land, such as clearing fields and constructing shelter.

+   Settlers faced attacks by Native American tribes on whose lands they traveled or settled.

The pioneers faced many hardships in the settlement of the West.

© 2005 ASCD. All rights reserved.

Given that many students tend to believe that learning simply involves the acquisition of knowledge and skills, these tools signal the kind of intellectual work required when understanding is the goal. Venn diagrams, comparison matrices, and similar graphic organizers are helpful in signaling the meaning-making goal and scaffolding the work. Although such strategic tools and teacher support are helpful to novices, be sure to wean students off these aids over time. Always keep in mind the long-term goal of autonomous transfer by the learner.

Here is a general sequence for such scaffolded instruction, in this case applied to a graphic organizer, but applicable to any similar tool or strategy:

1. The teacher shows the students a completed organizer for the day's lesson.
2. She provides examples for students to study.
3. The teacher models how to use the organizer, using a think-aloud process to reveal her thinking.
4. She involves the students in using the organizer, providing guided practice and feedback as they work. Increasingly, students work independently in applying the organizer to diverse and more sophisticated uses.

Equipping for Performance

Another aspect of equipping learners is to plan backward from the desired transfer tasks. Thus our design work in Stage 2 is germane here. It is one thing to present a goal statement to a class; it is quite another to walk through the companion performance task and rubric that will reveal knowledge, understanding, and proficiency.

Yet even when the tasks are known, few students will be able to perform at high levels if they do not also know what expected performance looks like in concrete terms. This point underscores the importance of providing not only the evaluative criteria (rubrics) but also tangible models of the desired results.

Here is a note on models: it is tempting to simply show students one example of an excellent product or performance. Two common problems may occur as a result of showing a single example:

- Some students will simply copy it. This runs counter to our intent—that is, thoughtful and original performance, not thoughtless imitation.
- Others, especially lower-achieving or less confident students, will view the model as way beyond their capacity and simply shut down and not try.

To avoid these occurrences, we strongly recommend that you show a range of models, illustrating *excellent, good, fair,* and *poor* performances. By studying a range of samples, students are more likely to have a vision of what's possible, better understand the key traits and evaluative criteria, and be able to self-assess as they work.

When particular products (e.g., a museum display) and performances (e.g., a debate) are expected, students may very well need instruction, practice, and coaching on the qualities of the various genres. For example, reviewing the qualities of an effective museum display or showing videos of skilled debaters would be in order, especially if students are unfamiliar with these forms.

 Design Task: Given your unit goals and desired performances, what type of scaffolding will support learners in acquiring knowledge and skill, making meaning of big ideas, and transferring their learning? Figure K.5 provides examples of how to generate ideas for equipping students for performance.

R—Rethink, Revise, Reflect

How will students be guided to rethink their understanding of important ideas? How might student products and performances be improved through revision? How will students be encouraged to reflect on their learning and performance?

A central premise of Understanding by Design is that the big ideas must be regularly reconsidered so that prior understandings are challenged and initial understandings are deepened. Here is an example. A 1st grade class explores the essential question "What is friendship?" by discussing their experiences with

Figure K.5

WHERETO Worksheet—Examples for *E* (Equip for Performance)

Given your overall goals (Stage 1) and the proposed assessments (Stage 2), what knowledge and skills are needed to equip students for successful performance? Look at the example below; then use the worksheet to fill in your own ideas.

Performance Task or Other Evidence		
Assume the role of a historical character and role-play that person's participation in a debate on a current issue.		
To perform successfully, students will have to know • Rules of debate • Debate procedure *and be able to* • Succinctly state a position • Use rebuttal techniques	***THEN***	*What teaching and learning experiences will be needed to equip students for successful performance?* • Review the rules of debate • Show video excerpts of debates to illustrate the procedure and effective debating strategies • Teach rebuttal techniques

Performance Task or Other Evidence		
To perform successfully, students will have to know _____ _____ *and be able to* _____ _____	***THEN***	*What teaching and learning experiences will be needed to equip students for successful performance?* _____ _____ _____ _____

friends and reading various stories about friendship. Students develop a theory of friendship and create a concept web for the topic (making meaning). The teacher then prompts them to rethink their initial conception by posing a second essential question using a story about "fair-weather" friends—"Who is a *true* friend, and how do you know?" By rethinking their initial ideas (for example, a friend is someone you enjoying playing with), students modify their concept of friendship as they come to understand that a true friend is loyal during hard times, not just a playmate during happy times. Finally, the teacher further challenges students' thinking by presenting them with two proverbs—"The enemy of my enemy is my friend," and "A friend in need is a friend indeed"—and asks them to reexamine their theory of friendship yet again based on these ideas.

Design Task: Tried-and-true teaching techniques can stimulate rethinking, and Figure K.6 presents some of these for your consideration. Which of these might work for your unit?

Figure K.6

WHERETO—Examples for *R* (Rethink)

Review the various ideas to help learners rethink, revise, and reflect. Then check off those ideas that you will include in your learning plan.

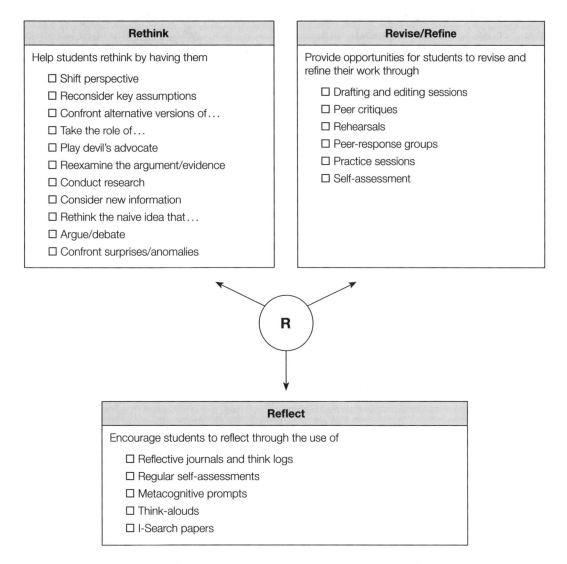

Rethink
Help students rethink by having them
☐ Shift perspective
☐ Reconsider key assumptions
☐ Confront alternative versions of…
☐ Take the role of…
☐ Play devil's advocate
☐ Reexamine the argument/evidence
☐ Conduct research
☐ Consider new information
☐ Rethink the naive idea that…
☐ Argue/debate
☐ Confront surprises/anomalies

Revise/Refine
Provide opportunities for students to revise and refine their work through
☐ Drafting and editing sessions
☐ Peer critiques
☐ Rehearsals
☐ Peer-response groups
☐ Practice sessions
☐ Self-assessment

R

Reflect
Encourage students to reflect through the use of
☐ Reflective journals and think logs
☐ Regular self-assessments
☐ Metacognitive prompts
☐ Think-alouds
☐ I-Search papers

Using the Facets for Rethinking

The six facets of understanding were originally conceived as indicators of understanding for use in assessment (Stage 2), yet they have proven to be a useful frame for prompting rethinking in Stage 3. You can use the six facets to brainstorm possible activities (mindful, of course, of the desired results of Stage 1 and the needed assessment evidence of Stage 2). The last three facets—perspective, empathy, and self-knowledge—are particularly useful for causing students to rethink. For example, shifting perspective from the American view to the French view of the Revolutionary War in America is an eye-opening way to remind learners that a worldwide battle for domination was going on in which the United States was a minor player. Asking students to empathetically walk in the shoes of different characters in a novel will likely cause significant rethinking. This is true even in science and mathematics: Einstein wondered as a high school student what he would see if he rode on a beam of light at the speed of light. That is "empathy" and "shift of perspective" that led to world-changing rethinking! Alternate geometries (besides Euclid's) were invented by shifting perspective about what we should assume to be true about parallel lines. And asking students to regularly reflect on how new learning affects their own views, and vice versa, will cause the activation and deepening of thought we all seek as educators.

➲ **Design Task:** Use the worksheet in Figure K.7 to brainstorm ideas for stimulating your students to rethink and revise, mindful of the six facets.

E—(Self-) Evaluate

How will students be guided in self-evaluation as they work? How will learners engage in a final unit reflection to identify remaining questions, set future goals, and point toward new learning? The second *E* in WHERETO underscores the vital role of metacognition in effective learning. Essentially, metacognition refers to the practice of deliberately reflecting on one's thinking and learning and monitoring the effectiveness of one's actions as one tries to learn or perform. Researchers point out that metacognitive abilities do not emerge spontaneously for most students. Thus teachers must signal their importance and cultivate them overtly:

> The teaching of metacognitive skills should be integrated into the curriculum in a variety of subject areas. Because metacognition often takes the form of an internal dialogue, many students may be unaware of its importance unless the processes are explicitly emphasized by teachers. (Bransford, Brown, & Cocking, 2000, pp. 18, 21)

The following are some simple examples of "designing in" metacognitive opportunities.

At the beginning of the year, have students develop a personal profile of their strengths and weaknesses as learners (perhaps through formal learning-styles instruments provided by the teacher). They should consider the following factors: how they learn best, what strategies work well for them, what type of learning is most difficult, and what they wish to improve (goal setting). Then structure periodic opportunities during the unit for journaling, when students can monitor their progress and reflect on their struggles and successes.

Figure K.7

Brainstorming Ways to Rethink and Revise Using the Six Facets

Use the six facets of understanding to generate possible learning activities that require students to *rethink* and *revise* earlier ideas.

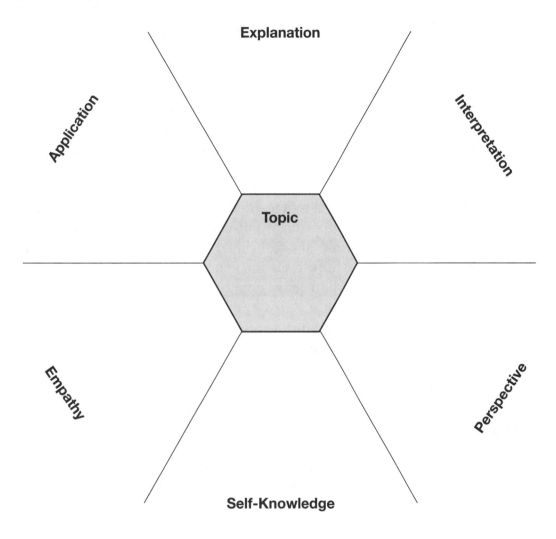

Set aside five minutes in the middle and at the end of an inquiry-based experience *(e.g., a laboratory experiment, Socratic seminar, or role-play) to consider questions such as these:* So, what have we learned? What remains unresolved and in need of further inquiry? (You can use K-W-L or a variant of it as well.)

Periodically assign a one-minute essay at the end of a class, in which students reflect and summarize the two or three main points and identify the questions that still remain for them (and, thus, next time, for the teacher!). A variation of this practice is called "think and draw," in which learners create a graphic representation of their learning and the connections that they have made.

Teach students to evaluate products and performances in the same way that teachers are trained to be judges in Advanced Placement or statewide writing assessments, so that students become more accurate as peer reviewers and self-assessors.

Occasionally videotape learners (e.g., during discussion, problem solving, experimentation, or debate), so that they become more cognizant of effective strategies, as well as what doesn't work (just as coaches have their players study game films).

Regularly use self-assessment prompts to have learners reflect on their learning and self-evaluate their performance. (Other examples appear in McTighe & Wiggins, 2004.)

Require that a self-assessment be attached to every formal product or performance, in which students describe their use of strategies and evaluate their performance. (Teachers may choose to base a small part of the student's grade on the accuracy of the self-assessment.)

Figure K.8 presents a practical tool to encourage student self-evaluation and goal setting. Notice that each cell of the rubric contains two boxes. Students can use one set of boxes (left) to self-evaluate their performance as they work. In fact, some teachers have established the expectation that students turn in the completed self-assessment rubric along with their assignment or product.

Once the assignment or task is scored by the teacher (using the same rubric) and returned, the student can compare the ratings. The student then completes the Goals/Actions section at the bottom of the rubric, based on the teacher's (and the student's own) evaluation. Over time, we would expect students to become increasingly capable of honest self-assessment and adjustment, without the teacher having to tell them how they did or what they need to work on. This practice signals that self-evaluation and goal setting is an expected part of a learner's job.

⮕ **Design Task:** Review the self-evaluation ideas presented in this section and insert appropriate ideas into your learning plan. Use the questions in Figure K.9 to further develop ideas for engaging your students in self-evaluation and reflection of their performance.

Self-Assessment—Review Criteria for Module K

The conclusion of the WHERETO discussion and the review criteria for the WHERETO elements appear at the end of Module M.

Further Information on the Ideas and Issues in This Module

Understanding by Design, 2nd ed. (Wiggins & McTighe, 2005). Chapter 9, pages 197–218. Read at greater length about the WHERETO elements and rationale, and review more examples of how designers can build and self-assess their learning plan using these elements.

Figure K.8

Rubric for Self-Assessment and Teacher Assessment—Persuasive Essay

Traits:		Persuasive	Clear	Thorough	Polished
Weight:		30%	30%	20%	20%
Scale	4	Very persuasive. Compelling evidence; sound reasoning, effective in countering opposing positions or arguments. ☐ ☐	Very clear. Position is precisely stated; the argument is easy to follow; persuasive language is targeted to audience. ☐ ☐	Very thorough. Rich and comprehensive detail provided to fully address the issues and support the argument. ☐ ☐	Very polished. No errors of syntax, mechanics, or usage. Publishable quality. ☐ ☐
	3	Persuasive. Solid evidence, generally sound reasoning; acknowledges other positions or arguments. ☐ ☐	Clear. Position is stated, the reader can follow the argument; language appropriate for targeted audience. ☑ ☐	Thorough. Sufficient detail is provided to address the issues and support the argument. ☐ ☐	Polished. A few minor errors of syntax, mechanics, or usage that do not detract from the overall effect of the essay, minor editing needed. ☑ ☐
	2	Somewhat persuasive. Some gaps in logic or reasoning; some evidence is missing and/or inappropriate; does not effectively counter other arguments. ☑ ☑	Somewhat clear. Position is somewhat vague or ambiguous; argument is implied but too hard to follow; language may not fit the audience. ☐ ☑	Somewhat thorough. Some detail is provided, but more is needed to adequately address the issues and support the argument. ☑ ☑	Somewhat polished. A few distracting errors of syntax, mechanics, and/or usage; editing and rewriting is needed. ☐ ☑
	1	Not persuasive. Illogical, missing, or inappropriate evidence; does not acknowledge other positions or arguments or evidence. ☐ ☐	Unclear. Writer's position is not evident; no coherent argument is provided; language is inappropriate for targeted audience. ☐ ☐	Not thorough. Insufficient detail provided; does not adequately address the issues and/or support the argument. ☐ ☐	Unpolished. Numerous errors in syntax, mechanics, and/or usage make the essay difficult to follow; significant editing and rewriting needed. ☐ ☐

Goals/Actions: Next time I write a persuasive essay, I'll do a little more research on the topic and think about what other people are going to argue (especially those who disagree with me). That's hard for me because I always think my views are just right! My writing is pretty good, but I know I need to add more details to support my views.

The Understanding by Design Guide to Creating High-Quality Units (Wiggins & McTighe, 2011). Module H discusses learning for understanding and how designers need to focus on honoring each of the three kinds of goals—transfer, meaning-making, and acquisition. There are extended examples on how to design this kind of learning.

Understanding by Design: Professional Development Workbook (McTighe & Wiggins, 2004). Pages 212–227. Comprehensive set of worksheets and examples for Stage 3 are provided, including further examples of WHERETO and worksheet prompts for designing one's own learning plan.

Schooling by Design: Mission, Action, and Achievement (Wiggins & McTighe, 2007). Chapter 5, "What's My Job When I Am with Students?" Describes the three roles of effective teachers: teacher of content acquisition, facilitator of meaning-making, and coach of performance. A set of common misunderstandings about teaching for understanding and responses to those misunderstandings are also provided.

References

Bransford, J., Brown, A., & Cocking, R. (Eds). (2000). *How people learn: Brain, mind, experience, and school* (Expanded ed.). Washington, DC: National Academy Press.

McTighe, J., & Wiggins, G. (2004). *Understanding by Design: Professional development workbook.* Alexandria, VA: ASCD.

Wiggins, G., & McTighe, J. (2005). *Understanding by Design* (2nd ed.). Alexandria, VA: ASCD.

Wiggins, G., & McTighe, J. (2007). *Schooling by design: Mission, action, and achievement.* Alexandria, VA: ASCD.

Figure K.9

WHERETO—Examples for the Second *E* (Evaluate)

The second *E* in WHERETO asks the designer to build in opportunities for ongoing evaluation, including opportunities for students to self-evaluate. The following questions may be used as prompts to guide student self-evaluation and reflection.

- What do you really understand about _____?
- What questions/uncertainties do you still have about _____?
- What was most effective in _____?
- What was least effective in _____?
- How could you improve _____?
- What would you do differently next time? _____
- What are you most proud of? _____
- What are you most disappointed in? _____
- How difficult was _____ for you?
- What are your strengths in _____?
- What are your deficiencies in _____?
- How does your preferred learning style influence _____?
- What grade/score do you deserve? Why? _____
- How does what you've learned connect to other learnings? _____
- How has what you've learned changed your thinking? _____
- How does what you've learned relate to the present and future? _____
- What follow-up work is needed? _____
- Other: _____

Module L

Sharpening Essential Questions and Understandings

Purpose: To refine and revise essential questions and understandings.

Desired Results:

Unit designers will understand that

- Crafting effective essential questions and genuine understandings requires ongoing self-assessment and revision by designers.

Unit designers will be able to

- Develop and revise high-quality essential questions and understandings, based on self-assessment and revision.

Module Design Goals: In this module, you will learn to distinguish between overarching and topical understandings and essential questions, and refine your unit essential questions and understandings.

You should work on Module L if your draft understandings and essential questions need polishing or they have not been reviewed against UbD design standards.

You might skim and return later to Module L if your essential questions and understandings have been reviewed and meet UbD design standards.

Although you might get the *meaning* of essential questions, it doesn't follow that you are able to *transfer* your understanding to write great essential questions on your own. Practice and feedback make perfect. Keep writing and tinkering, and before long you'll have good essential questions.

Essential Questions: Doorways to Inquiry

As noted in earlier modules, a question is *essential* if it meets the following criteria. For example, does the question

- Cause genuine and relevant inquiry into the big ideas of the core content?
- Provoke deep thought, lively discussion, sustained inquiry, and new understanding as well as more questions?
- Require students to consider alternatives, weigh evidence, support their ideas, and justify their answers?
- Stimulate vital, ongoing rethinking of big ideas, assumptions, and prior lessons?
- Spark meaningful connections with prior learning and personal experiences?
- Naturally recur, creating opportunities for transfer to other situations?

The best essential questions cause sustained inquiry. They pique interest, they focus thinking and discussion, and they help students connect, extend, and probe the content. Thus the challenge in crafting them is not so much to fuss endlessly with their wording as to aim for effect. In other words, the purpose of an essential question is more important than its form.

As discussed in earlier modules, devising good essential questions is more difficult than it first seems—not because writing such questions is challenging from a wordsmithing perspective but because teachers are prone to ask factual or otherwise leading ("teacherly") questions. So the first challenge in polishing our draft questions is to make sure that we are focused on opening up student inquiry instead of converging on the content we want learned.

The important point is that the best essential questions are those that become the *students'* questions over time. The best questions evolve from being one that a teacher asks to one that thoughtful people consider on their own. It isn't until the learners "own" the question so as to proactively explore issues and challenges as they arise that we have succeeded as designers and teachers. In the more general language of UbD, the best essential questions facilitate transfer and make students increasingly independent as thinkers and learners the more *the students* ask them when appropriate (versus only when prompted to by others). This point is concretely underscored in the UbD Template (see also Wiggins & McTighe, 2011, Module F). Designers are asked to identify essential questions, not essential answers as a desired result in Stage 1. Here are some examples of such questions:

- Who is my audience, and what follows for what I say and how I say it?
- What is likely to happen next? (in reading a text or making predictions)
- What should I do when I am stuck or fearful of making a mistake?
- What am I wasting and how can I waste less?
- How much power should leaders have?

- Have I understood? What should I do when I am unsure?
- What does this remind me of?
- Why am I reacting this way? Is there a better way to react?
- Which parts of me and my life are given, and which parts of me am I free to change?
- Who is a true friend? How can I tell?
- How can I turn this problem into something more familiar and easier to work with?
- What is this person trying to communicate?
- How much debt should I/we/the nation take on?
- Why do people move?

Notice that these questions are broad in scope. Indeed, they can apply to more than one grade level, and many are applicable to various subject areas. Notice, too, that some of the questions are about issues, whereas others are about strategy. Finally, note that these questions usefully recur over time; they never become moot or easily answered with finality. Indeed, answers may well evolve over a lifetime. In short, essential questions focus on meaning (as the UbD Template signifies), whereas typical knowledge questions point toward facts. Figure L.1 can help you distinguish between essential questions and knowledge questions.

Figure L.1

Essential Questions Versus Knowledge Questions

Essential Questions	Knowledge Questions
1. Are meant to be explored, argued, and continually revisited.	1. Have a specific, straightforward, unproblematic answer.
2. Have various plausible answers. Often the "answers" raise new questions.	2. Are asked to prompt factual recall rather than to generate a sustained inquiry.
3. Should provoke thought and stimulate students to engage in sustained inquiry and extended thinking.	3. Are more likely to be asked by a teacher or a textbook than by a curious student or person out in the world.
4. Reflect genuine questions that real people seriously ask, either in their work or in their lives—not "teacherly" questions asked only in schools.	4. Are more rhetorical than genuine.

Note: There is a distinction between concrete "hook" questions (e.g., *Can what you eat help prevent zits?*) intended to engage students' interest in a new topic, and more transferable essential questions (e.g., *Must food that is good for you taste bad?*). We recommend placing hook questions in Stage 3 as part of the learning plan.

Editing Essential Questions

Because the ability to craft good essential questions is a learned skill and because many teachers have difficulty relinquishing the idea of their questions as a prelude to acquisition of knowledge, very few people create a perfect essential question on the first try. We have found it helpful to think of designing essential questions as a genre of writing, and like the writing process itself, it's a genre that typically requires multiple drafts and revisions, based on self-assessment and (where possible) peer feedback. Study the sets of before and after essential questions in Figure L.2 to see examples of revisions and associated comments.

Figure L.2

Revising Essential Questions

Original Draft Questions	Commentary on the Drafts	Revised Questions	Commentary on the Revisions
Are there any benefits from the deforestation of the rain forests?	*The question calls for some research/information gathering and analysis but ends in a list.*	Do the benefits of deforestation outweigh the costs?	*The revised question broadens the inquiry and calls for a more sophisticated analysis; it's far more likely to spark debate and deeper inquiry than any list of pros and cons.*
How does this diet match up with the USDA nutrition recommendations?	*The question requires some analysis and evaluation, but it can be answered correctly.*	What should we eat?	*This is a much more open version with lots of potential for inquiry and debate.*
What is nonfiction?	*This is a definitional question that can be answered unambiguously.*	How much license does a writer of nonfiction have to make a point?	*This version of the question explores an interesting gray area having both historical and contemporary relevance.*
What is a life-changing experience?	*Although somewhat open, this question can be answered through recall and surface thinking.*	Is there a pattern to life-changing experiences?	*This revised question calls for learners to make inferences about the concept of "life changing."*
Who speaks Spanish in our community?	*This is a nonproblematic question asking for a list.*	How well can you thrive speaking only English?	*This more provocative version calls for greater analysis and a shift of perspective.*
What is an axiom?	*This is a definitional question calling for a straightforward answer.*	Why should we assume that [an axiom] is true?	*This much more open question gets at why some things are "given" even if they do not seem obvious or necessary.*
What distinguishes impressionism art?	*This is a leading question with an expected set of characteristics.*	Why and how do artists break with tradition?	*These questions require an examination of artistic trends and a generalization by the learner.*
What types of exercises will improve fitness?	*This question involves research but is leading. The answers are straightforward.*	"No pain, no gain"—agree?	*The revised version is more provocative and likely to spark discussion, debate, and further inquiry.*

Do you notice what is common to the revisions? They move away from being leading or factual questions toward being more open and nuanced. The revised versions imply that there is a range of plausible answers or that a thoughtful judgment has to be made. They all call for inquiry and extended thinking, and answers are likely to be refined or even rethought as inquiry unfolds and understanding deepens. Note also that the original questions might be used as part of the investigation but are not the best for framing the whole inquiry.

Editing essential questions thus involves asking yourself how to make a question more inviting of a range of answers or thoughtful qualifications to answers based on judgment. Some simple linguistic moves are available for doing this if you aren't satisfied with your current draft. The following phrases open up a question and invite a wider range of possible answers: *To what extent...? How important is...? In what ways might...? What would happen if...? Why...? Under what conditions...? On balance, is...?*

Some essential questions are "guiding" in that they are initially open to many plausible interpretations and answers, but they *eventually* end in an understanding. Many essential questions in the sciences—*What are things made of?, Where does the water go?, Why do things move the way they do?*—fit this description. Nonetheless, such questions can guide student inquiry, stimulate thinking, and encourage meaning-making by the learner.

Keep in mind that the wording of the question may not be the decisive element in determining its capacity to engage thinking—despite what you might have been taught about the use of yes/no questions. In fact, some phrasings that seem leading on the surface can work well to generate and sustain lively inquiry and debate. Consider, for example, *Is biology destiny?* or *Is conflict inevitable?* Both questions issue an invitation to discuss and debate (supported, of course, by the right instructions and guidelines; for example, we would quickly make clear that a mere yes or no response from students is unacceptable). Such questions and initial answers would be followed by probes (e.g., *Why do you think that? Who has a different idea or reason?*) or devil's advocate challenges (e.g., *But how would you respond to those who would say...?)* to keep thinking alive.

On the other side, some seemingly open-ended questions (e.g., *What were the most important causes of the Civil War? When is it OK—perhaps even desirable—to speak ungrammatically?*) are really not open if the textbook or teacher, after a brief discussion, tells you *the* answer and sends the clear message that the issue is settled. Regardless of the phrasing of the question, the core issue in unit design and implementation is making it clear that the *intent* of the question is to have sustained inquiry. Meaning-making, not acquisition, is the point of an essential question.

Design Task: Examine the essential questions for your unit in light of the previous discussion and exercises. Are all identified essential questions open-ended, likely to provoke thought and inquiry, and point toward important understandings? How might your questions be edited to best suggest the kinds of inquiry and range of answers you are looking for students to achieve?

Overarching Versus Topical Questions

You might also have noticed that some of the questions we have cited (as well as your own, perhaps) are of varying scope. Some questions are overarching; that is, they extend across many units (and courses, sometimes). Other essential questions are more topical or unit specific. Good design, in part, involves nesting the more specific questions under the larger questions so that students begin to see how course content is interrelated and how a few powerful questions can help focus and synthesize their learning. Although in practice no firm boundaries separate topical and overarching questions, the following differences can be noted. Overarching questions

- Are broad and general in nature. They point beyond a single unit to larger, transferable ideas and issues. Practically speaking, the specific topics, events, or texts of the unit are typically not mentioned in the framing of overarching questions. For example, the question "What makes a book 'great'?" is an overarching question that can be addressed throughout the entire English/language arts program.
- Link two or more units together. For example, "Whose story is it?" can be fruitfully posed in many social studies units across the grades (as well as in science and English/language arts).
- Link implicitly to other overarching questions. Given the example of an overarching question mentioned in the first bullet, a topical question for a unit might then be "Is *Stranger in a Strange Land* great literature or just a good read?" The overarching question "What makes a book great?" might also link to others; for example, "How do effective writers hook and hold their readers?"

Topical questions, in contrast,

- Refer specifically to the unit topic.
- Can be addressed quite thoroughly via the content within a particular unit.

Although they are narrower in scope, we do not mean to suggest that essential questions in a unit have a single, "correct" answer. Rather, there may be several plausible answers that are defensible from the facts of the unit. In other words, we want even our topical questions to promote inquiry and discussion, and to engage student thinking. Figure L.3 presents additional examples to help you distinguish the two question types.

In general, we propose that overarching questions (and companion understandings) be used to map the curriculum at the course and program levels. These broad questions can then be focused more specifically to explore unit topics. (More information about the role of overarching understandings and essential questions can be found in Chapter 3 of *Schooling by Design*, Wiggins & McTighe, 2007).

Figure L.3

Overarching Versus Topical Questions

Overarching Questions	Topical Questions
These questions point beyond the particulars of a unit to the larger, transferable big ideas and enduring understandings. Practically speaking, the specific topics, events, or texts of the unit are typically not mentioned in the framing of overarching questions. For example, *Is science fiction great literature?* is an overarching question for any unit on a specific text such as *Stranger in a Strange Land*.	Topical questions are subject- and topic-specific. They frame a unit of study. They guide the exploration of big ideas and processes within particular subjects. For example, *What aspects of* Stranger in a Strange Land *are plausible?* is a question that guides inquiry within a specific literature unit. This unit question links to the overarching question *How "true" is a fictional story?*, which is addressed within other English/language arts units.
Examples	
Art • In what ways does art reflect culture as well as shape it? • How do artists choose tools, techniques, and materials to express their ideas? **Literature** • What makes a great story? • How do effective writers hook and hold their readers? **Science** • How does an organism's structure enable it to survive in its environment? • How do organisms survive in harsh or changing environments? **Mathematics** • If axioms are like the rules of the game, when should we change the rules? **History/Government** • How do governments balance the rights of individuals with the common good? • How and why do we provide checks and balances on government power?	**Unit on masks** • What do masks and their use reveal about the culture? What tools, techniques, and materials are used in creating masks from different cultures? **Unit on mysteries** • What is unique about the mystery genre? • How do great mystery writers hook and hold their readers? **Unit on insects** • How do the structure and behavior of insects enable them to survive? • How do insects survive when their environment changes? **Unit on the parallel postulate** • Why is this an axiom if it's so complex? • What no longer holds true if we deny it? **Unit on the U.S. Constitution** • In what ways does the Constitution attempt to limit abuse of government powers? • Does separation of powers (three branches of government) create a deadlock?

Using Essential Questions

Developing engaging essential questions in Stage 1 that point toward desired understandings can be challenging, but it's just the first step. In Stage 3 we are challenged again to *use* the questions effectively to help students make meaning of important ideas and processes. Although there is much to say about the instructional use of essential questions, here are a few recommendations.

Use a reasonable number of questions (two to five) per unit. Having a few good questions helps to prioritize the content for students, especially when the same questions are revisited throughout the unit.

Introduce essential questions through concrete experiences or personal examples. For example, a discussion of the abstract principle of "property rights" is made quickly accessible and intriguing by asking students whether "finders keepers" is OK, perhaps enlivened through a role-play exercise. Then larger, more essential questions about property naturally arise (How do we come by a right to property? What are the arguments for and against private property? When can property be legitimately transferred, and when is that right abused—for example, by downloading music from the Internet without paying?).

When necessary, frame the essential questions in "kid language," as needed, to make them more accessible. Edit the questions to make them as engaging and provocative as possible for the age group.

Post the essential questions prominently in the classroom and refer to them regularly. This signals to students that their job is to continually consider these important questions. Get them in the habit of referring back to the essential questions at stake in any concrete reading, experience, problem, or lesson.

Use the questions for ongoing assessment; that is, have students summarize their thinking about the question periodically throughout the unit. Doing so enables you and the learners to see evidence of deepening understanding and more nuanced thinking over time.

Consider using the essential questions as part of summative assessment. In this case, students' responses are evaluated as evidence of their meaning-making.

Revising Our Understandings

If essential questions frame ongoing and important *inquiries* about the issues and challenges in a subject, understandings reflect important *answers*—stated as full-sentence generalizations—that we want our students to eventually "see" after seriously considering the questions. Here's an example: The essential question "Why is that *there*?" sets up a serious and ongoing inquiry into a big idea that perhaps "geography is destiny." As a result of exploring the question and related idea, we want students to come to specific understandings—generalizations based on inference—such as the following:

- Human needs for food, work, commerce, and transportation often determine where people settle and cities grow.
- The geography, climate, and natural resources of a region influence how people live and work there.

Notice that these understandings are not limited to a particular region or city. They are transferable across time and location in ways that facts are not. So the big idea of "geography as destiny" can be transported to any new location to help us better understand culture, history, economy, and politics. Figure L.4 offers further clarification and paired examples of understandings versus knowledge (facts) on various topics.

Figure L.4

Understandings Versus Knowledge

Understandings	Knowledge
• Are supportable conclusions—valid inferences based on facts and reasoning. • Aren't so much right or wrong as relatively more or less defensible and in depth. • Can vary across individuals and in ourselves over time as new evidence, arguments, and reflection dictate. • Are meaningful and transferable ideas and strategies. • Lead to the discovery or development of new knowledge.	• Is accurate information that we acquire. • Is either correct or incorrect. • Is established by settled and uncontroversial methods. • Is useful information that causes and results from successful inquiry. • Provides the facts in support of any rational understanding.
Paired Examples	
a. In a free-market economy, price is a function of supply and demand. b. Statistical analysis and data display often reveal patterns that may not be obvious. c. The most efficient and effective stroke mechanics in swimming involve pushing the maximum amount of water directly backward. d. Heating of Earth's surface and atmosphere by the sun drives convection within the atmosphere and oceans, producing winds and ocean currents.	a. The price of long-distance phone calls has declined during the past decade. b. Mean, median, and mode are measures of central tendency. c. The freestyle is an event in which the fastest times in swimming occur. d. Winds can sometimes exceed 200 miles per hour.

We often ask workshop participants to consider their understandings as the "moral" of the unit "story" as opposed to the details. You can see how this works with one of Aesop's fables:

The Ant and the Chrysalis

An Ant nimbly running about in the sunshine in search of food came across a Chrysalis that was very near its time of change. The Chrysalis moved its tail, and thus attracted the attention of the Ant, who then saw for the first time that it was alive. "Poor, pitiable animal!" cried the Ant disdainfully. "What a sad fate is yours! While I can run hither and thither, at my pleasure, and, if I wish, ascend the tallest tree, you lie imprisoned here in your shell, with power only to move a joint or two of your scaly tail." The Chrysalis heard all this but did not try to make any reply. A few days after, when the Ant passed that way again, nothing but the shell remained. Wondering what had become of its contents, he felt himself suddenly shaded and fanned by the gorgeous wings of a beautiful Butterfly. "Behold in me," said the Butterfly, "your much-pitied friend! Boast now of your powers to run and climb as long as you can get me to listen." So saying, the Butterfly rose in the air and, borne along and aloft on the summer breeze, was soon lost to the sight of the Ant forever.
Moral: Appearances are deceptive.

Note that the moral is more general than the particulars of the fable. This is a crucial aspect of learning with understanding: we learn to generalize beyond the facts and use those inferences to transfer prior learning to new situations.

So what's the moral of the story of World War II in a history unit? What's the generalizable lesson from studying the particulars of fractions and decimals? The answers reflect the kind of useful generalizations that we term "understandings" in UbD.

A couple of additional points about understandings are worth noting. First, once an understanding becomes second nature, it becomes so obvious to us that we easily treat it mistakenly as a fact. (Naive professors and teachers are prone to this mistake, as are parents!) But you came to understand it by a chain of reasoning, not by mere inspection or acquisition. Second, just because someone says "Well, that's *my* understanding!" doesn't mean that the understanding is valid. It may be based on weak evidence and faulty logic.

So, how can you get your desired understandings to "excellent" from "just OK"? Just because you have come up with a full-sentence generalization related to your unit topic doesn't guarantee that you have identified a genuine understanding worth learning. Some identified understandings are really just truisms, vague notions, or facts. To help you critically review your Stage 1 understandings (and, if necessary, edit them), review the examples and revision ideas in Figure L.5.

Understandings and Misunderstandings

A simple rule of thumb about understandings is that they are prone to common misunderstandings. That's what makes them not so obvious and not truisms. So it is always wise to consider the most likely student *mis*understandings when teaching for understanding, designing the assessments in Stage 2, and framing the understandings in Stage 1. Figure L.6 provides some illustrations of possible misunderstandings.

Topical and Overarching Understandings

We previously discussed differences in the scope of essential questions, and similar distinctions apply to desired understandings. Some understandings are comprehensive in nature, whereas others are more specific. Here, too, we distinguish between topical and overarching.

As with topical and overarching essential questions, no hard and fast rule is available for distinguishing topical from overarching understandings. The scope of the course content, subject matter priorities, age of students, time allotted to the unit, and other factors will influence the breadth and depth of the targeted understandings. Rather than thinking of the difference as one of absolute size or scope, it is best to think of the overarching understandings as representing the transferable

Figure L.5

Revising Understandings

Original Draft Understandings: *Students will understand that*	Commentary on the Drafts	Revised Understandings	Commentary on the Revisions
The three branches of government.	*This phrase simply states the topic, not the understanding sought about that topic. Note the stem (Students will understand that…), which is designed to remind you of this need.*	Our founders believed in *limited and divided* government, in order to ensure that absolute power could never occur in government.	*The revised understanding is both a transferable generalization and a not so obvious result of analysis of the history of monarchies and dictatorial regimes.*
We should eat right and live healthy lives.	*This understanding is a truism—obvious on its face and not requiring thought beyond basic knowledge to grasp.*	We are what we eat.	*The revision is a more thought-provoking and focused understanding that should encourage discussion and further inquiry in order to uncover the insights in the statement.*
Different countries have different cultures.	*Although this is an understanding that may not be obvious to younger students, the claim is so vague that it isn't clear where this leads in terms of specific inquiry and insight.*	Cultures develop unique traditions and norms around universal human needs (e.g., food and housing) and experiences (e.g., celebrations and mourning).	*The revised understanding provides greater focus about the inquiry and learning in the unit, and hints at an important paradoxical insight: cultures develop differently around universal human needs and experiences.*
Force makes things move.	*This is too superficial and imprecise a statement of the desired understanding.*	$F = ma$	*Newton's law is a profound, concise, and focusing understanding.*
Factoring and regrouping are ways to simplify.	*This is true by definition and doesn't get at the powerful idea in mathematics as to why we want to simplify and how in general to do it.*	Solving problems requires simplifying expressions by finding useful equivalent statements by which unknowns and unwieldy expressions are easier to work with.	*The revised understanding, although wordy, summarizes a critical idea about how all problem solving depends in part on finding equivalences.*
Artists are always working to be creative.	*This is a somewhat superficial view of the artistic process. It doesn't really suggest an in-depth or interesting inquiry about the creative process.*	"Creativity is 10 percent inspiration and 90 percent perspiration" (Pasteur).	*The revised version is a concise but profound and (to many) counterintuitive claim about the role of hard work in the creative process.*
Many linear relationships can be found in the world.	*This statement is extremely vague—we aren't told where to find such relationships or how. As stated, it is more of a fact than a useful insight drawn from inference.*	If you find a relationship in which two variables are related to each other in a constant ratio, the relationship can be represented graphically by a straight line.	*The revised understanding, although abstract, accurately describes the general class of relationships called "linear" and how to find them. (Note that this is not true by definition; it must be inferred from the definition and experience with such relationships.)*

Figure L.6

Anticipating Misunderstandings

Use these examples to help you identify possible misunderstandings for identified understandings or skills.

Desired Understanding	Possible Misunderstanding
Friendship is often revealed more through challenging times than during happy times.	People with whom you "hang" are your friends. Once a friend, always a friend.
Gravitational force is the only significant force acting on a ball once it has been thrown.	When a ball is thrown by the pitcher, there are two forces acting on it as it travels toward the catcher.
States' rights issues, linked to regional economies, were a cause of the Civil War, but historians now generally agree that the chief cause was the economics and ethics of slavery.	The Civil War was fought over the evil of slavery, and the "good guys" won.
...for a Skill Area	**Possible Misunderstanding**
Listening is not passive. Effective listeners actively monitor their understanding of the speaker's message by summarizing, clarifying, and questioning.	All I need to do is sit still, keep my eyes on the speaker, and hear all of the words.
Solving problems requires constantly clarifying the goal and the givens.	The math problem tells you how to solve it.
The author of a story rarely states a purpose or meaning, so readers have to infer them.	The meaning of the story is found in the text.

List possible misunderstandings for your identified understandings or skills.

Desired Understanding	Possible Misunderstanding

insights eventually sought. In other words, given the specific unit understandings you desire, to what extent can those insights be generalized, to serve the student with connective powers in other work? Put the other way around, what recurring ideas should be framing your coursework, of which the topical understanding is this unit's embodiment? Figure L.7 presents additional examples to help you distinguish the two types of understandings.

As the sets in Figure L.7 indicate, understandings can be nested, based on different degrees of abstraction or generalization. The understandings in the first column are more general than their partners in the second, which point beyond the particulars of the topic or unit of study toward more transferable knowledge. These overarching understandings (in the first column) also help address the common

Figure L.7

Overarching Versus Topical Understandings

Overarching Understandings	Topical Understandings
These understandings point beyond the specifics of a unit to the larger, transferable insights we wish students to acquire. They often reflect yearlong course or K–12 program understandings. The specific topics, events, or texts of the unit are typically not mentioned in the overarching understandings.	Topical understandings are subject- and topic-specific. They focus on the *particular* insights we wish students to acquire about the topic within a unit of study. Topical understandings are less likely to transfer naturally to other topics.
Examples	
Art • Art often reflects the controversial, overlooked, or taboo aspects of a culture; or novel techniques and media.	**Unit on Impressionism** • Impressionist artists departed from traditional painting forms by using color, light, and shadow to convey the impression of reflected light at a particular moment.
Literature • The modern novel overturns many traditional story elements and norms to provide a more authentic and engaging narrative.	**Unit on *Catcher in the Rye*** • Holden Caulfield is an alienated antihero, not simply a weird kid who mistrusts adults.
History/Government • Democracy requires a free and courageous press, willing to question and investigate authority.	**Unit on the U.S. Constitution** • The Watergate incident, exposed by the press, represented a major constitutional crisis.
Mathematics • Mathematics allows us to see patterns that might otherwise have remained unseen.	**Unit on statistics** • Measures of central tendency enable us to find the right "average."
Physical Education • A muscle that contracts through its full range of motion will generate more force.	**Unit on golf** • A full stroke with follow-through will increase the distance a golf ball travels.
Science • Gravity is not a physical thing but a term describing the constant rate of acceleration of all "falling" objects.	**Unit on gravitational force** • Vertical height, not the angle and distance of descent, determines the eventual speed of a falling object.

student questions "Why do we have to learn this?" and "So what?" about work that seems to have no larger purpose. The examples in the second column are topic-specific insights. We refer to them as topical understandings. They identify the particular understandings we hope to cultivate about specific topics.

Understandings and Skill

As we noted with essential questions, it is a misconception to think that there are no big ideas in skill-focused teaching. In subjects such as reading, writing, mathematics, world languages, vocational courses, and physical education that emphasize skill development, the understandings can be typically found in the strategies, rationale, or value of the skills. Here's a skill-related understanding for sports (e.g., throwing a baseball or football, swinging a golf club, throwing darts): *When you "follow through" (in your throw or stroke) you generate greater power and control than if you do not.* Such an understanding enables students to practice the skill (being mindful of following through) while monitoring its effects. Just as coaches and teachers encourage such mindful practice in athletics, teachers can similarly cultivate skill-based understandings in academic areas.

Design Tip: In skill areas, the understandings most often reflect the *rationale* for a strategy and thus generalize about best practice. Take a strategy and provide the rationale for it. For example, if the strategy is "Keep your eye on the ball," the rationale might be this: "Most novice athletes lose eye contact when they swing, without realizing it. You need to keep your eye on the ball by taking deliberate action to be looking at it all through your swing." If you teach in skill areas and are having difficulty identifying appropriate understandings for your unit, try the worksheet shown in Figure L.8.

Figure L.8

From Skills to Understandings

Review the following examples of big ideas and understandings related to skills. Then brainstorm possible understandings related to skills for your unit.

Stated as a Skill ——▶	Underlying Big Ideas ——▶	Specific Generalizations to Be Understood
Swimming: mechanics of arm strokes (freestyle, backstroke, breaststroke, butterfly, side stroke)	• Efficiency • Maximum power • "Backward" push • Surface area	• The most efficient and effective stroke mechanics push the maximum amount of water directly backward. • A flat (versus cupped) palm offers the maximum surface area. • A bent arm pull enables a swimmer to push water directly backward with greatest power.
Adding fractions	• Part to whole relation • Relating "likes" to "likes"	• When "parts" are combined, they have to be framed in terms of the same "whole."
Ideas for Your Unit		

Working with Understandings

Arguably one of the more difficult aspects in teaching for understanding is to decide whether to or when to directly teach the understanding. In other words, to put it as an essential pedagogical question, When should you state the understanding and when should you engineer students to come up with it "by design"? Whether we consider the famous example of Socrates in his *Dialogues* or some of the best teachers we have ever had as students, many of them had the ability to help us discover the understanding on the basis of their clever design groundwork, their probing, and their facilitation of discussion.

That said, we are not advocating for a one-size-fits-all approach to instruction. In fact, we have all had experiences in the other direction, as teachers or parents. Sometimes we say the same thing, over and over, and on the umpteenth time the learner may say, "Oh, I see! So *that's* what you meant!" Note the language: just because we said it doesn't mean they see what we mean. An understanding has to be seen by the learners themselves; it has to be an insight that they grasp with our assistance. Naive teachers, by definition, think that understanding is transmitted like factual knowledge—as if it were obvious (when, in fact, it is not obvious to novices). When you feel yourself getting frustrated as a teacher and either thinking or saying "Don't you see this?" you can bet that you have not laid sufficient groundwork and facilitated enough dialogue and reflection to put students in a position to get it.

In other words, one of the great *teacher* misunderstandings is that we need only tell the understanding for true understanding to occur. On the contrary, as mystery stories, movies, and (especially) video games reveal, not only is the learner perfectly capable of drawing appropriate inferences, but such activity is key to increasing intellectual engagement, autonomy, and reducing the boredom of schooling. And ironically, the literature on student misconception reveals that in spite of clear teaching of big ideas, many students do not understand what they have been taught (even if they pass our quizzes).

Here, then, are some tips for aiming at student ownership of understandings in the classroom and on the basis of assignments:

Use a reasonable number of understandings (one to four) per unit. Since an understanding serves, in effect, as the moral of the unit, there simply cannot be too many for the experience to be coherent or manageable. Initially in your teaching you may want to practice aiming for only one understanding per unit to get a feel for the kind of groundwork and probing that needs to be laid for the understanding to occur in students by design.

Help students practice drawing inferences from facts. Most students think that the point of learning is to take in and give back (or even regurgitate) the facts presented by teacher and text. Take a page from the work of Taffy Raphael and others (Raphael, Highfield, & Au, 2006) in reading, and signal early and often to students (until they really get the distinction!) that some answers are found on the page and others are found in your head. For example, Socratic seminars and problem-based learning are instructional approaches designed so that the learner must construct meaning, not wait for the teacher to simply tell or give the answers.

Before teaching the unit, decide if the understandings will be helped or compromised by being stated or posted early on. No hard and fast rule governs this point; it is usually determined on a case-by-case basis. Nonetheless, ask yourself if the understanding, as phrased, will likely be completely meaningless or seemingly unhelpful until the students "see" its meaning. If so, you lose little by stating and repeating it, and your students will likely gain quicker understanding. However, if in stating the understanding you would completely undermine the inquiry, discussion, and testing of ideas needed to really "get it," then you probably should not state the understanding until the teachable moment when it serves as a concise summary of what students have come to see or just said. Then, if others didn't follow the inference, you can now take them (or have students take them) through the logic that leads to the generalization.

Because an understanding is typically a fairly general or abstract inference, encourage students to keep notes or use organizers of the facts, experiences, and claims that build toward their understanding. For example, graphic organizers can help students construct meaning from a collection of facts and textual information.

Because an understanding is a fallible inference, it is important to strengthen student understanding by considering alternative understandings (including seductive misunderstandings) if you want the understanding to really take hold in the students' minds. We know from the research on concept attainment that understanding demands looking at multiple, contrasting cases/examples/claims whenever there is an abstract idea to learn. That's why debates—where students are required to consider counterexamples and counterarguments—are often very effective (as well as engaging) in causing deeper understanding. You can build multiple and differing points of view into scenarios in both instruction and via GRASPS (see Module M) in assessments.

➲ **Design Task:** Examine the understandings for your unit in light of the previous discussion and exercises. How might your understandings be edited to best summarize the important inferences that you want students to make and the insights you hope they will attain? How might your Stage 3 be modified to make it likely that the work builds toward genuine insight on the part of students?

Self-Assessment—Review Criteria for Module L

Use the following criteria to self-assess your current unit design:

- Is the content of the unit framed around transferable big ideas (concepts, themes, issues/debates, processes, problems, challenges, theories, assumptions)?

- Are the identified understandings based upon transferable big ideas?
- Are the desired understandings stated as full-sentence generalizations in response to the stem *"Students will understand that…"*?
- Are all of the Stage 1 elements (established goals, understandings, transfer goals, essential questions, knowledge, and skills) appropriately connected?

Further Information on the Ideas and Issues in This Module

Understanding by Design: Professional Development Workbook (McTighe & Wiggins, 2004). See the following pages in particular: page 91 for characteristics of essential questions; pages 93–104 for additional examples of essential questions and skills; page 106 for tips on using essential questions; pages 108–110 for additional examples of understandings ("meanings"); and page 118 for understandings in skill areas.

Understanding by Design, 2nd ed. (Wiggins & McTighe, 2005). Extended discussions of big ideas and essential questions are found in Chapters 5 and 6.

Schooling by Design: Mission, Action, and Achievement (Wiggins & McTighe, 2007). Chapter 3 includes a discussion of overarching understandings and essential questions, and their role in mapping the curriculum at the program and course levels.

References

McTighe, J., & Wiggins, G. (2004). *Understanding by Design: Professional development workbook.* Alexandria, VA: ASCD.

Raphael, T., Highfield, K., & Au, K. (2006). *QAR now: A powerful and practical framework that develops comprehension and higher-level thinking in all students (theory and practice).* New York: Scholastic.

Wiggins, G., & McTighe, J. (2005). *Understanding by Design* (2nd ed.). Alexandria, VA: ASCD.

Wiggins, G., & McTighe, J. (2007). *Schooling by design: Mission, action, and achievement.* Alexandria, VA: ASCD.

Module M

....

Authentic Assessment and Validity

....

Purpose: To refine Stage 2 by establishing authenticity (via GRASPS) and validity.

Desired Results:

Unit designers will understand that

- Authentic assessment tasks call for real or simulated performances reflecting how people use knowledge and skill in the world beyond school.

- The GRASPS elements help designers create contextualized, real-world tasks. Students often find authentic tasks more relevant and engaging than typical tests.

- In addition to authentic tasks, valid assessment of all Stage 1 elements typically requires evidence of a more traditional kind.

Unit designers will be able to

- Develop authentic performance tasks to validly assess Stage 1 goals, especially those related to transfer and meaning.

- Check for validity of Stage 2 assessments against Stage 1 goals.

Module Design Goals: In this module, you will refine your Stage 2 performance tasks by using the GRASPS elements to frame an authentic context for each. Additionally, you will complete your Stage 2 plan by specifying the *other evidence* needed to assess all the goals of Stage 1. Finally, you'll assess your Stage 2 plan to ensure that the listed assessments provide valid evidence for all stated Stage 1 goals. The end product will be a more complete unit plan, including authentic assessment tasks and other assessment evidence for all of the desired results identified in Stage 1.

You should work on Module M if you have not already established an authentic context for your assessment tasks, or have not fully assessed all of your Stage 1 goals.

You can skip over Module M if you have authentic tasks reflecting the GRASPS elements or know how to create them, and all Stage 1 goals are appropriately assessed in Stage 2.

....

In previous modules, we have explored long-term goals that involve transfer, considered evidence of understanding, and developed assessment tasks based on the six facets. Now we offer ways in which you can fine-tune the performance task ideas by establishing an authentic context.

Authentic Tasks

The long-term purpose in schooling is transfer: to equip learners to take what they have learned and use it outside school (Wiggins & McTighe, 2011). In other words, we want students to be able to apply what they know flexibly and effectively to address new and realistically contextualized issues and problems. With this end in mind, we recommend that teachers set up genuinely rich and realistically messy contexts for many unit and course assessments, for it is when students are able to apply their learning thoughtfully and flexibly under real-world conditions that true understanding is demonstrated. A benefit is that such tasks tend to be more meaningful and motivating for students.

Establishing an authentic context is not just interesting for learners but vital for transfer ability. A sports analogy applies here. During practice, coaches run drills under simplified conditions to help players develop and refine specific skills. The game differs from practice, however, in that it is inherently quite unpredictable and higher-order. Players are faced with ever-changing situations and decisions. They must transfer the skills and knowledge they have practiced, which is different from replicating a sideline drill. To make transfer easier, coaches include regular scrimmages during practice to simulate game conditions and then debrief what worked, and what didn't work, and why.

What happens in athletics should happen in schools, though it often does not. In classrooms we see an overemphasis on tests and worksheets that are the equivalent of decontextualized sideline drills, with few if any opportunities for students to actually play the game or "do" the subject in realistic ways and to gain feedback and insight from attempts to perform. Down the road, the performance of those who only practice with drills invariably suffers in the face of genuine performance demands, even on external standardized tests in which students typically encounter novel questions requiring them to transfer prior learning.

Examples of Authentic Tasks

What is the nature of authentic assessment? What's the difference between "drill" and "game" assessments in school? Figure M.1 compares these differences for various subjects.

The examples of authentic tasks in Figure M.1 should make clearer what we mean by realistically messy tasks. In such tasks, the student has to navigate the vagaries of context, including such things as personalities, audience demands, available resources, and distractions. Again, this is not just to make the task more interesting but to increase its validity, because understanding requires transfer to new, realistic, and unscripted situations.

Figure M.1

Authentic Tasks Versus Simplified Exercises

Simplified (Drill-like) Exercises	Authentic (Gamelike) Tasks
Select an answer from given data.	Interpret data based on real-world phenomena.
Fill in the blank with a recalled fact, or answer from someone else's research.	Conduct research using primary and secondary sources.
Recall what the history book says on a controversial issue.	Engage in a simulated debate on a controversial historical issue in a simulated United Nations session.
Answer factual questions at end of the chapter in a chemistry textbook.	Conduct a scientific investigation to identify unknown chemical compounds.
Solve simple, contrived math problems that have a single correct answer.	Solve real-world math problems that have multiple solution paths and different plausible answers.
Identify the topic sentence.	Interpret the meaning and assess the value of an award-winning children's novel.
Diagram sentences.	Write for a real audience with an explicit purpose (e.g., to entertain or persuade).
Copy a famous drawing.	Create a political cartoon to satirize a current event or policy.

Consider the authentic demands in the following tasks:

Mythic Job Search—Students practice writing and job-search skills in the context of a literature unit, working from the following instructions: Select an epic hero from the literature we have read, and write a letter to the hero in which you apply for a job as a crew member on his expeditions. In the letter, you must be specific about the position for which you are applying, your qualifications for the job, and why you feel you would be an asset to the crew. Be sure to make your letter persuasive by making it clear you understand the particular struggles and adventures the hero and crew have already undertaken, and how you might be of value to them in handling such situations and difficulties. Write in business letter form, and include a résumé.

Water Treatment—"How can we sell new lakeside houses next to dirty lakes? We've got to clear the sediment in this water, but we also must save the fish!" With this challenge in mind and after reading memos from an environmental lab describing a problem with sediment in five area lakes, student teams will propose a solution to the problem. In addition to the science content and processes, the task also assesses students' problem-solving, communication, and teamwork skills.

But What Was Going on Here?—Fourth graders interview local residents as they conduct an oral history of the era of the civil rights movement, following these instructions: The personal side of local history can quickly disappear as those who experience it move or die. To ensure that our local area does not lose its sense of what happened during the civil rights movement of the 1950s and 1960s, you will be part of a writers' project to capture the memories of these times. You, as a researcher, will interview a member of your family or a friend of your family who lived in [your town or city] during the period between the Rosa Parks bus incident and the death of Martin Luther King Jr. Record the interview, make a transcript of it, and then write a brief summary that characterizes the incidents and feelings in the interview. This material will be forwarded to the high school history class where students, based on your interview and other information they will uncover in their research, will be writing the history. It will be important to the high school students that your summary be informative and accurate.

Shipping M&M's—Students design a cost-effective container for shipping candy in bulk, following these instructions: You work for the company that makes and markets M&M's. Recently a large chain of candy stores ordered several tons of M&M's. They want the candy shipped to them in containers that can be used to forward shipments by truck and rail to stores in their chain. These stores all sell candy by the pound, so the candy as it is currently packaged in individual packets does not work. Further, the competition for this sale was so great that your company had to cut its profit to the bare minimum.

To help with this low profit margin, you and two of your colleagues have been assigned the task of coming up with the least expensive packaging possible—one that minimizes the material required to produce the package while maximizing the amount of candy that can be safely and efficiently packaged and shipped. Your supervisor has found an inexpensive source for the material to be used in making the package—flat, rectangular poster board. You have been given a sample of this material in the size that it comes in.

Your job is to (1) design and build a container that, in shape and dimension, will hold the largest volume of M&M's for safe and economical shipping; (2) prepare a written report to your supervisor, making the case for your design and supplying all appropriate data and formulas.

As with every job in your department, your supervisor will be persuaded by your mathematical insight and reasoning, the quality of your report, the accuracy of your findings, and the effectiveness and inventiveness of the solution.

Investigating Claims—Students learn to consider claims in written material, following these instructions: The Pooper Scooper Kitty Litter Company claims that their litter is 40 percent more absorbent than other brands. You are a consumer advocate researcher who has been asked to evaluate their claim. Develop a plan for conducting the investigation. Your plan should be specific enough as well as scientifically valid so that the lab investigators could follow it to evaluate the claim.

Authentic assessments such as these have two virtues associated with understanding-related goals: (1) realistic tasks call for students to apply their learning thoughtfully and flexibly, thereby providing stronger evidence than normal about students' understanding and ability to transfer; and (2) authentic tasks provide clear, worthy, and valid intellectual goals that help learners see a reason to make an effort to prepare for them.

Design Tip: Think of traditional quizzes and tests as the equivalent of sideline drills. Such exercises test your ability to handle one or two skills or sets of facts at a time, out of context. These are labeled as Other Evidence on the UbD Template. But the game is quite different. It demands *conditional* knowledge; that is, a key challenge is to figure out which skills and knowledge to use, and when to use them. That is the essence of a test of understanding in real life. Such assessments require transfer in context and are placed under the Performance Tasks section of the Template in Stage 2.

For example, in the unit on nutrition, students should learn about the food groups, nutritional values of various foods, the USDA recommendations for a balanced diet, and health problems that can result from poor nutrition. This knowledge, although important, is not an end in itself; the longer-term transfer goals call for students to be able to make healthful eating decisions and plan balanced diets for themselves and others when they are on their own, faced with various realistic complexities, such as a limited budget and preparation time.

Misconception Alert

To call for authentic assessment is not to demand that a task be simply fun or interesting or hands-on. The task must be as authentic as possible to better embody Stage 1 goals. Worrying only about whether a task is engaging runs the risk of sacrificing validity for fun. This harkens back to the two-question validity test originally posed in Module D (Wiggins & McTighe, 2011):

- Could students do the proposed assessment(s) well but not really have mastered or understood the content in question?
- Could students do poorly on the specific assessment(s) but really have mastery of the content in question?

Authentic Task Frames

So, what does playing the game look like in the subject areas? The task frames in Figure M.2 present generic ideas for transfer tasks in various disciplines. The frames function as springboards from which ideas for more specific tasks can be developed. Note that these frames support the design of recurring tasks across the grades.

Now consider the contextual aspects of such task frames. Because transfer demands flexible performance in ongoing novel tasks and situations, we should in different assessments vary the audience, the setting, the degree of prompting provided, the resultant products or performances, and other factors to gauge over time students' ability to transfer their learning flexibly as well as fluently. For example, over time students would be expected to persuade not just their friends but their adversaries; be required to convince a venture capitalist to fund an idea during a 30-second elevator pitch, as well as convince an academic audience of the same idea in a formal seven-page proposal. The following are examples of how the same task frame can be used to generate recurring tasks for different grade levels.

Task Frame
Interpret the data on _____ for the past _____ (*time period*).
Prepare a report _____ (*oral, written, graphic*) for _____ (*audience*) to help them understand

- What the data show.
- What patterns or trends are evident.
- What might happen in the future.

Primary Grade Task: Second grade students in three separate classes work in teams of four and take turns measuring the height of each team member, using tape measures affixed to the classroom walls. The height measurements are taken at the beginning of the school year and every seven weeks thereafter. When they begin, the 2nd grade teachers and classroom aides model the process and assist the youngsters with their measurements and their recordings. As the year progresses, the students require less help with the task, and by year's end, many groups are working completely independently.

By mid-May, each 2nd grade class has obtained six height measurements since the start of the school year. The teachers demonstrate how to create a simple graph with height in inches plotted against the months of the school year, and the students plot their own data. Using rulers, they connect the dots to see "rise over run" (a visual representation of their growth over time).

The chart papers are posted throughout the room, and the students circulate in a gallery walk to view the changes in heights of the various groups. The teachers then ask the students to analyze the data by posing guiding questions: *In what months did we grow the most this year? Is there a difference between how boys and girls have grown in 2nd grade? How does our class growth compare to the growth in the other 2nd grade classrooms?* (The teachers create an "Average Class Growth" chart that they show to all the 2nd graders.) *What can we predict for next year's 2nd graders about how they will grow based on our data?* The students are then asked to work in their groups to develop a presentation for the current 1st graders.

Figure M.2

Performance Task Frames

English Language Arts

☐ Read and respond to *text in various genres* (literature, nonfiction, technical) using
- Global understanding (the "gist").
- Interpretation (reading between the lines).
- Critical stance.
- Personal connections.

☐ Create *oral presentations* or *written* pieces in various *genres* for various *audiences* in order to
- Explain (narrative).
- Entertain (creative).
- Persuade (persuasive).
- Help perform a task (technical).
- Challenge or change things (satirical).

☐ Use various *sources* (e.g., lecture, radio commercial) for various *purposes,* including for
- Learning.
- Enjoyment.
- Performing a task.
- Reaching a decision.

Mathematics

☐ Create a mathematical model of physical phenomena (e.g., quantity, size, rate, change).
☐ Conduct data analysis, specifically
- Observe.
- Collect.
- Measure.
- Record.
- Display.

☐ Make and justify predictions based on pattern analysis.
☐ Design a physical structure (e.g., a three-dimensional shipping container to maximize volume and safety).
☐ Evaluate mathematical/statistical claims.

Science

☐ Design and conduct an experiment to answer a question or explain phenomena.
☐ Effectively use scientific tools to
- Observe.
- Collect data.
- Measure.
- Record data.
- Classify.
- Draw conclusions.

☐ Evaluate scientific claims.
☐ Critique experimental design or conclusions.
☐ Analyze current issues involving science or technology.

History/Social Studies

☐ Evaluate historical claims or interpretations based on conflicting and incomplete information from
- Primary source.
- Secondary source.
- Personal opinion.

☐ Critically analyze current events/issues:
- Summarize/compare key points.
- Analyze causes and effects.
- Identify points of view and potential bias.
- Debate possible courses of action.

☐ Make informed decisions using critical thinking and understanding of historical patterns.
☐ Act as a responsible citizen in a democracy (e.g., stay informed, study issues, participate in community events, vote).

Visual and Performing Arts

☐ Create artistic expressions through various forms:
- Media (e.g., pastels, photography).
- Genre (e.g., jazz music, modern dance).
- Styles (e.g., Impressionism, cubism).

Figure M.2—(*Continued*)

Performance Task Frames

Visual and Performing Arts—(*continued*)

☐ Create artistic expressions for various audiences and purposes, including to
   • Entertain (e.g., tell a story).   • Persuade.
   • Evoke emotion.   • Challenge (e.g., the status quo).
   • Commemorate.
 	
☐ Respond to artistic expressions through
   • Global understanding.   • Critical stance.
   • Interpretation.   • Personal connections.

Health and Physical Education
☐ Engage in healthful activities and behaviors to promote wellness throughout life. ☐ Make healthful choices and decisions about diet, exercise, stress management, and substance abuse.
Foreign/World Languages
☐ Understand spoken and written communications in the target language. ☐ Communicate effectively (orally and in writing) in the target language in realistic situations.

Secondary Grade Task: High school students use several Internet search engines to locate data from the World Health Organization, the National Institutes of Health, and at least two other sources on documented cases of H1N1 influenza (also known as swine flu) beginning in March 2009. Working in teams, the students engage in the following tasks activities:

- Collect and record data from at least four sources on the spread of H1N1 virus in various countries.
- Compare and evaluate the sources (e.g., *Which sources were the most thorough? The most understandable? The most credible?*).
- Analyze the data (e.g., *What patterns did you notice in rates of infection related to age and gender? Geographic spread? Associated deaths? Impact of governmental policies, such as travel restrictions or quarantine, on the spread of infections? Predictions of future spread?*).
- Prepare a summary report to effectively communicate the data and your analysis to a target audience (e.g., congressional committee, general public, teenagers) using an appropriate communications medium (e.g., newspaper article, blog, website, podcast, TV news special). Include recommendations (e.g., for government policy or individual precautions) in the event of a future outbreak of a different flu strain.

The GRASPS Elements

Once the basic performance idea has been identified, we encourage designers to frame the task with features suggested by the acronym GRASPS as a means of creating more authentic applications of understanding. The tasks should include (1) a real-world **G**oal, (2) a meaningful **R**ole for the student, (3) an authentic (or simulated) **A**udience, (4) a contextualized **S**ituation that involves real-world application, (5) student-generated culminating **P**roducts and Performances, and (6) the performance **S**tandards (criteria) for judging success.

GRASPS Applied to the Nutrition Unit

To see how the GRASPS frame can help, let's apply it to two of the performance task ideas in the nutrition unit. Notice the difference between the basic task and the version framed using GRASPS:

Task 1—Students will develop a brochure that they can use to explain what "balanced" eating is and what health problems can develop from poor nutrition.

Task 1 Framed with GRASPS—Because our class has been learning about nutrition, the 2nd grade teachers in our elementary school have asked our help in teaching their students about good eating. Your task is to create an illustrated brochure to teach the 2nd graders about the importance of good nutrition for healthful living. Use cut-out pictures of food and original drawings to show the difference between a balanced diet and an unhealthy diet. Show at least two health problems that can occur as a result of poor eating. Your brochure should also contain accurate information and should be easy for 2nd graders to read and understand.

Task 2—Students will develop a meal plan and reference the food groups and USDA recommendations.

Task 2 Framed with GRASPS—Because we have been learning about nutrition, the camp director at the Outdoor Education Center has asked us to propose a nutritionally balanced menu for our three-day trip to the center later this year. Using the USDA food guidelines and the nutrition facts on food labels, design a plan for three days, including the three main meals and three snacks (a.m., p.m., and campfire). Your goal is a healthy and tasty menu. In addition to your menu, prepare a letter to the director explaining how your menu meets the USDA nutritional guidelines. Include a chart showing a breakdown of the fat, protein, carbohydrates, vitamins, minerals, and calories. Finally, explain how you have tried to make your menu tasty enough for your fellow students to want to eat.

Figure M.3 shows a task organized within the GRASPS framework.

Note that the GRASPS versions of the task is derived from the original ideas, but it is more detailed, contextualized, and personal. GRASPS helps establish a realistic context, or situation (S), including a clear goal (G), role for the student (R), and audience (A). Additionally, the learners work on authentic products or performances (P), judged against performance standards (S).

Design Task: Use the blank version of the GRASPS worksheet in Figure M.4 to help frame one or more of your unit assessment tasks. Remember that the design challenge is to create a realistic context for student performance.

Figures M.5 and M.6 provide sample roles, audiences, products, and performances. These lists can spark ideas for authentic tasks.

Figure M.3

Performance Task for Nutrition—GRASPS Example

Goal:

The goal (within the scenario) is to create a menu for the three-day trip to the Outdoor Education Center.

Role:

You are a menu advisor.

Audience:

The target audience is the Outdoor Education Center director (and your peers).

Situation:

You need to propose a nutritionally balanced and tasty menu, within budget, for three days of camping by the entire class.

Product/Performance and Purpose:

- Menu plan for three days, including the three main meals and three snacks (a.m., p.m., and campfire).
- Letter to the director explaining how your menu meets the USDA nutritional guidelines. Include a chart showing a breakdown of the fat, protein, carbohydrates, vitamins, minerals, and calories. Explain how you made your menu as tasty as possible.

Standards and Criteria for Success:

- Healthy and tasty menu
- Well-written and well-supported letter

Comments on the GRASPS Elements

Although the elements of GRASPS are straightforward, we offer commentary on each element to help you avoid various misconceptions.

Goal—The goal refers to the student's aim in the scenario, not the teacher's intent or the unit goal. For example, the goal for the student in the nutrition task (Figure M.3) is *to learn how to plan a nutritionally balanced and tasty menu*, whereas the teacher's goal for the assessment is to obtain evidence that students understand healthy, balanced eating and can support their understanding with a well-written letter.

Role—What role should students play in the scenario? The decision should relate primarily to the assessment evidence you need, given your Stage 1 goals. Thus it makes sense for the role to require students to *explain* (e.g., teach a younger child) or *apply* (e.g., create a menu plan) to show their understanding. Be careful not to establish roles that are unrelated to the understanding goals so that you are not asking students to use skills and knowledge that are not relevant to the unit.

In some cases, mindful of the "perspective" and "empathy" facets of understanding, it may be worthwhile to allow students to take different roles in the same

Figure M.4

GRASPS Task Scenario Builder

Consider the following set of sentence starters as you construct a scenario for a performance task.
Note: These are stems to help you generate ideas. Resist the urge to fill in all of the blanks.

Goal:
- Your task is _____.
- The goal is to _____.
- The problem or challenge is _____.
- The obstacles to overcome are _____.

Role:
- You are _____.
- You have been asked to _____.
- Your job is _____.

Audience:
- Your clients are _____.
- The target audience is _____.
- You need to convince _____.

Situation:
- The context you find yourself in is _____.
- The challenge involves dealing with _____.

Product or Performance and Purpose:
- You will create a _____
  in order to _____.
- You need to develop _____
  so that _____.

Standards and Criteria for Success:
- Your performance needs to _____.
- Your work will be judged by _____.
- Your product must meet the following standards _____.
- A successful result will _____.

scenario. Consider the following example: "You are a plantation owner, legislator, abolitionist, preacher, or factory owner just before the Civil War. Your job is to express your view about secession in a simulated town hall debate." A related option is to have students shift roles in different phases of the scenario. In the Civil War example, for instance, you might have each student play a specific role related to the secession debate and then switch to being a newspaper editor to write an editorial on the issue. In a science or mathematics task, students could develop a design and proposal for a skateboard park. In the second phase, they could play the role of the Parks and Recreation Board to review all the design proposals.

Figure M.5

Possible Student Roles and Audiences

O = ROLES   □ = AUDIENCES

O □ actor	O □ family member	O □ playwright
O □ advertiser	O □ farmer	O □ poet
O □ artist/illustrator	O □ filmmaker	O □ police officer
O □ author	O □ firefighter	O □ pollster
O □ biographer	O □ forest ranger	O □ radio listener
O □ board member	O □ friend	O □ reader
O □ boss	O □ geologist	O □ reporter
O □ Boy/Girl Scout	O □ government official	O □ researcher
O □ businessperson	O □ historian	O □ reviewer
O □ candidate	O □ historical figure	O □ sailor
O □ carpenter	O □ illustrator	O □ school official
O □ cartoon character	O □ intern	O □ scientist
O □ cartoonist	O □ interviewer	O □ ship's captain
O □ caterer	O □ inventor	O □ social scientist
O □ celebrity	O □ judge	O □ social worker
O □ CEO	O □ jury	O □ statistician
O □ chairperson	O □ lawyer	O □ storyteller
O □ chef	O □ library patron	O □ student
O □ choreographer	O □ literary critic	O □ taxi driver
O □ coach	O □ lobbyist	O □ teacher
O □ community member	O □ meteorologist	O □ tour guide
O □ composer	O □ museum director/curator	O □ trainer
O □ client/customer	O □ museum goer	O □ travel agent
O □ construction worker	O □ neighbor	O □ traveler
O □ dancer	O □ newscaster	O □ tutor
O □ designer	O □ novelist	O □ TV/movie character
O □ detective	O □ nutritionist	O □ TV viewer
O □ editor	O □ panelist	O □ viewer
O □ elected official	O □ parent	O □ visitor
O □ embassy staff	O □ park ranger	O □ website designer
O □ engineer	O □ pen pal	O □ zookeeper
O □ expert (in _____)	O □ photographer	O □ _____
O □ eyewitness	O □ pilot	O □ _____

© 2004 ASCD. All rights reserved.

Figure M.6

Possible Products and Performances

What student products and performances will provide appropriate evidence of understanding and proficiency? The following lists offer possibilities. (Remember that student products and performances should be framed by an explicit purpose or goal and an identified audience.)

Written	Oral	Visual
O advertisement	O audiotape	O advertisement
O biography	O conversation	O banner
O book report/review	O debate	O cartoon
O brochure	O discussion	O collage
O collection	O dramatic reading	O computer graphic
O crossword puzzle	O dramatization	O data display
O editorial	O interview	O design
O essay	O oral presentation	O diagram
O experiment record	O oral report	O diorama
O historical fiction	O poetry reading	O display
O journal	O puppet show	O drawing
O lab report	O radio script	O flyer
O letter	O rap	O game
O log	O skit	O graph
O magazine article	O song	O map
O memo	O speech	O model
O newscast	O teach a lesson	O painting
O newspaper article		O photograph
O play		O poster
O poem		O PowerPoint presentation
O position paper		O questionnaire
O proposal		O scrapbook
O research report		O sculpture
O script		O slide show
O story	Other:	O storyboard
O test	O _____	O video
O website	O _____	

© 2004 ASCD. All rights reserved.

Audience—As we know from writing, the audience matters. To make assessment tasks more authentic, consider the following questions: Who is the audience in the scenario? Who must the student-performer convince, inform, or entertain? Having the student focus seriously on what the particular audience needs and expects in particular situations is an important part of transfer—and real-world effectiveness.

In some cases, we can allow the students to select a target audience as long as their choice makes sense in the situation and will yield the needed evidence. Also, varying the audience in different phases of the same scenario can be an effective way to develop and reveal understanding.

Situation—The situation or setting establishes the context for task performance. We encourage designers to strive to create an authentic situation within which students will demonstrate their understanding. Note that we are using the term *authentic* in three senses:

- Authentic to the way in which people in the real world use the knowledge and skill students are learning;
- Authentic in terms of the opportunities and distractions inherent in real-world settings; and
- Authentic to the learner, in terms of relevance and personal interest.

The best tasks are authentic in all three senses. Here is an example from a mathematics unit on measures of central tendency:

> Your math teacher will allow you to select which measure of central tendency—*mean, median,* or *mode*—will be used to calculate your quarterly grade. Review your grades for quizzes, tests, and homework to decide which measure of central tendency will be best for your situation. Write a note to your teacher explaining *why* you selected that method.

As you think about your performance tasks, consider the following questions: How do people in the real world use the knowledge and skill students are learning? Under what conditions (e.g., options, opportunities, and impediments) is the student performing? How complex or realistically noisy is the context? For example, you know people speak with accents and different degrees of speed and precision of diction in many languages. Are your students encountering the range of such speech, or are they exposed only to the pure versions found in idealistic settings?

Most important, in the real world, people are expected to perform on their own without handholding. Clearly, the fewer hints, directions, and other supports provided, the more demanding the task is for students—that is, the more they have to innovate, self-assess, and self-adjust along the way. This observation suggests that educators need to design tasks that require an increasing level of student autonomy over time.

In Figure M.7 we show how you might increase or decrease the demands of the same task by varying the situation. Use Figure M.8 if you need help thinking of realistic situations and problems.

Product/Performance—The *P* in *GRASPS* asks designers to consider the specific products or performances that will provide evidence of the targeted understanding. When considering possible products and performances, we remind you to always keep the end in mind: The goal is not to simply come up with cool tasks, but to generate appropriate evidence of attaining targeted goals.

A teacher experienced with designing GRASPS tasks offers this helpful maxim: "If you don't control your *P*, you can lose your *G*." In other words, don't let the products and performances distract from the goal. It is critical to make this point clear to students. Otherwise they may put lots of effort into creating a pretty poster or dressing up for a role-play and lose sight of the purpose of the product or performance.

Figure M.7

Easier/More Difficult Situations

French Class

Easier Situation

"You need to make train reservations for a trip from Marseilles to Paris on the TGV. . . ." (The teacher is the ticket agent and speaks clearly, slowly, and repeats the words as often as requested when putting students in simulations of speaking with a ticket agent at a train station in Paris.)

More Difficult Situation

The teacher speaks quickly, with an accent, from behind a fake ticket window that makes it hard to hear. Impatient passengers wait behind the student to get their tickets as the loudspeaker in the station blares and other distractions are evident.

Language Arts Class

Easier Situation

"Write a letter to your principal about what can be done to lower utility costs in the school." (The teacher reminds students repeatedly of the steps in the writing process and provides graphic organizers for their draft letters.)

More Difficult Situation

The teacher says nothing about the writing process and reminds students that they only have 45 minutes in which to draft a letter to the principal about lowering utility costs before she has to leave for a board meeting.

Math/Science Class

Easier Situation

"Hoops McGinty has pledged a million dollars for a new museum dedicated to the solar system. The building lot is 300 × 800 feet. How would you design the layout of the main hall to fit a scale model of the solar system?"

More Difficult Situation

"Hoops has pledged the money under one condition: A regulation NBA basketball is to be used to represent a sun or a planet. The building lot is 300 × 800 feet. As a designer, how do you propose that the main exhibit hall with a model of the solar system be built to scale? If it cannot be done properly, what is your alternative approach to the design, to satisfy Hoops's interest in a basketball theme?"

Figure M.8

Brainstorming Realistic Situations

The following sentence starters and ideas can help you brainstorm realistic situations to use for GRASPS tasks. Consider the following situational elements: setting with opportunities and constraints, points of view, messiness, cost versus benefit, dilemmas, and trade-offs.

- Typical approaches won't do here. Content must be creatively used to _____.
- The different points of view here include _____.
- To succeed, you must overcome messiness such as noise, distractions, false leads, misleading information, missing information, or _____.
- Success depends upon thinking through the trade-off of _____ and _____.
- No solution is perfect here; the dilemma requires you to negotiate _____.
- You realize that you can't fully trust the advice of _____.
- In this setting it isn't clear if _____ has the knowledge or authority to _____.
- You may not have the resources you need to _____.

When it comes to assessment, we are "format agnostic." It doesn't matter whether it comes from writing, speaking, drawing, role-playing, or another activity *as long as the format permits us to gain the evidence needed* to assess the understandings and other goals identified in Stage 1. For example, if we want to see if students understand the water cycle and environmental factors that affect it, they could show their understanding via a written, visual, or spoken explanation. An exception, of course, is a unit in which the targeted standards involve, say, writing. In that case, at least one task has to be designed so that all students write. A drawing or an oral response would not provide a valid measure of that particular standard.

Standards (Criteria)—By what criteria will student process, performance, and products be evaluated—mindful of the Stage 1 goals being assessed? Against what standards, expectations, or degree of difficulty will the work be assessed? The challenge here is twofold: to make the criteria valid (given the purpose of the assessment) and to make completely clear to students the expectations of high-quality work.

A common weakness in performance assessments is the use of arbitrary criteria (as we discussed in Module J). For example, saying to students that a persuasive proposal must include "three reasons in support of their views" and "two footnotes" is arbitrary and inauthentic. In real life you are judged on the quality of the persuasion, not by the number of sources used. So the phrasing would be rewritten like this: "Your proposal has to provide convincing evidence and reasoning to persuade your audience. Make sure to include citations of sources used in support of your argument."

A more subtle criterion-related problem involves a tendency to evaluate the quality of the product or the performance instead of the depth of the student's ideas. Put differently, your scoring rubrics should highlight the understanding (and other Stage 1 results) sought and not simply fixate on the surface features of the specific products or performances being employed in the task.

Other Evidence, Revisited

We have long made the case for using performance tasks involving one or more of the six facets when we want to assess for understanding and transferability (Wiggins & McTighe, 2005). Moreover, we have proposed the use of GRASPS to create an authentic context for at least some of the tasks. This discussion of authenticity and GRASPS often raises an understandable concern: "Are you saying that all of our assessments must be framed this way?" Of course not.

Not all of our Stage 1 goals require complex performance tasks. Often, more efficient and familiar assessment methods will do. All such assessments go under Other Evidence on the UbD Template in Stage 2 (see Wiggins & McTighe, 2011). Just like a photo album typically contains a variety of pictures—some close-ups, some wide-angle shots, some focused portraits, and some including many people—so should our Stage 2 album include a variety of assessments matched to our goals. The logic of backward design rules here: the best assessments are the ones that provide valid evidence of the desired results.

If you can appropriately assess a Stage 1 goal with a more efficient assessment format (such as selected-response, brief constructed response), then do so. Reserve the GRASPS tasks for the most important transfer goals and understandings that are worth the extra time and effort. A teacher friend offers a helpful aphorism here. She says that with performance tasks, "the juice must be worth the squeeze." We need to make sure that the time required of students and teachers in both preparation and implementation is time well spent. On the other hand, constantly postponing authentic assessment deprives the student of clarity about transfer of the goal, as well as the motivation that typically comes from authentic tasks.

Additional online resources for this module include the following worksheets with prompts to help you. Figure M.9, Check: Is Every Desired Result Assessed?; Figure M.10, Matching Stage 1 Goals to Various Assessment Methods; Figure M.11, GRASPS Performance Task Scenario for Social Studies; Figure M.12, A Collection of Assessment Evidence (Nutrition Unit); Figure M.13, Design Checklist—Stage 2; Figure M.14, Assessment Design Tips and Guidelines.

Self-Assessment—Review Criteria for Module M

Review your current Stage 2 design against the following self-assessment questions. Revise as needed.

- Are the major performance tasks in Stage 2 framed in an authentic manner using the GRASPS elements?
- Does the other evidence provide valid and sufficient assessment evidence of the various goals identified in Stage 1?

Further Information on the Ideas and Issues in This Module

Understanding by Design, 2nd ed. (Wiggins & McTighe, 2005). Chapter 7 includes more information on "thinking like an assessor" and how to use GRASPS and the six facets of understanding to frame both valid and authentic performance assessments.

Schooling by Design: Mission, Action, and Achievement (Wiggins & McTighe, 2007). Chapter 5 describes the three roles of effective teachers—as teachers of content acquisition, as facilitators of meaning-making, and as coaches of performance. A set of common misunderstandings about teaching for understanding and responses to those misunderstandings are also provided.

Understanding by Design Professional Development Workbook (McTighe & Wiggins, 2004, pp. 154–174). Includes a comprehensive set of practical worksheets and examples for Stage 2, the six facets of understanding, and GRASPS.

The Understanding by Design Guide to Creating High-Quality Units (Wiggins & McTighe, 2011). Module G discusses assessing for understanding (meaning-making and transfer), the two-question validity test, and brainstorming tools for developing tasks based on the six facets of understanding.

References

Wiggins, G., & McTighe, J. (2005). *Understanding by design* (2nd ed.). Alexandria, VA: ASCD.

Wiggins, G., & McTighe, J. (2007). *Schooling by design: Mission, action, and achievement.* Alexandria, VA: ASCD.

Wiggins, G., & McTighe, J. (2011). *The Understanding by Design guide to creating high-quality units.* Alexandria, VA: ASCD.

Module N

Differentiating— Tailoring the Learning Plan to the Learners

Purpose: To develop unit plans that are tailored to the needs of individual learners.

Desired Results:

Unit designers will understand that

- The most effective curriculum designs are tailored to the learners they are meant to serve.

- Only certain aspects of a UbD unit should be differentiated.

- Pre-assessments and formative assessments provide information to enable teachers to adjust instruction to meet the needs of all learners.

Unit designers will be able to

- Tailor (differentiate) their unit plan to respond to the learners they serve.

- Include pre-assessments and formative assessments in their unit design.

Module Design Goals: In this module, you will refine your Stage 3 learning plan by incorporating ideas for differentiation to address the nature and needs of your students.

You should work on Module N if you have not yet (1) planned for differentiation or (2) included pre-assessments and formative assessments.

You might skip Module N if you have planned for differentiation and included pre-assessments and formative assessments as part of your Stage 3 learning plan.

In Module K we considered the WHERE elements and their implications for the Stage 3 learning plan. In this module we examine the first of the two remaining letters of WHERETO—*T* for *Tailoring* the learning to the learners—and an associated set of questions: *How will my unit design address the differing levels of readiness, learning profiles, and interests of my students? What's the best way to motivate a reluctant, timid, or detached learner to produce his or her best work?*

Considering the Learners

Until now you have probably been designing units for a somewhat generic class of students. Now the question becomes more contextualized: *How can I make my unit work with this particular group of students?* It is time to shift from thinking about what we want to accomplish as the teacher-designer to thinking about who the actual learners are—the end users of our unit design—and what they need, individually and collectively, to achieve the desired results of Stage 1 and to perform well at the tasks proposed in Stage 2.

Consider a simple analogy. The alpha version of software is designed just to get all the basic code working. The beta version involves testing with real users for usability. Like a software designer, we have to do more than ensure that all the features of the unit are going to work properly. We must ensure that the *users* of our design (our students) will be maximally engaged and productive. In other words, unit design, like good software, must be truly user-friendly, not just defensible in the abstract. That means attending to the learners and adjusting the unit design accordingly.

Making this admirable goal difficult, of course, is the likelihood that your students have fairly different needs, interests, and abilities. How, then, should your unit plan reflect that diversity? How much flexibility have you built into the draft unit, and how might you build in more—without compromising the unit goals (or driving yourself crazy with variations)? In the first part of this module we consider differentiation options in general through the lens of backward design and the UbD Template. Then we examine the use of pre-assessments and ongoing assessments in Stage 3 to inform needed differentiation of our unit plan.

Differentiation and Backward Design

Although we want our curriculum plan to be responsive to the diverse learners we serve, not everything in a UbD unit should be differentiated. As we design with both content and students in mind, the UbD Template can helpfully inform those aspects of our unit that may be differentiated and those that should not. With this point in mind, let's consider, stage by stage, the following question: what and when should we differentiate?

In Stage 1 of backward design, we identify desired results, including relevant content standards and other established goals, long-term transfer outcomes, and related big ideas that we want students to come to understand via essential questions. If appropriately and defensibly selected, these various goals should remain a constant target for *all* students, despite differences in students' background knowledge, interests, and preferred ways of learning. (The obvious exceptions involve students with individualized education plans. The particular goals of the IEP is added to, or substituted for, the course-level or grade-level expectations.) The goals are the goals, regardless of where we start. In other words, the transfer goals, big ideas, and related essential questions provide the conceptual pillars that anchor meaningful learning, and we do not arbitrarily amend these based on whom we are teaching in a course or grade level. (Of course, the nature and needs of learners should certainly influence how we teach toward these targets.)

The more specific knowledge and skill objectives in Stage 1 are linked to the desired standards and understandings—yet some differentiation may well be needed here. Because students typically vary in their prior knowledge and skill levels, responsive teachers tailor their instruction to address significant gaps in content. Such responsiveness follows from effective pre-assessments that reveal if gaps or misconceptions exist and formative assessments that reveal a need for some reteaching. Thus there is a place for sensitivity to student needs in Stage 1 without compromising the established standards or the integrity of subject areas.

In Stage 2, the logic of backward design dictates that we collect appropriate assessment evidence derived from the goals identified in Stage 1. Although the needed evidence, in general, is determined by these desired results, the *particulars* of an assessment can be differentiated to accommodate the uniqueness of students. For example, consider a social studies standard that calls for learners to analyze the causes and effects of a major historical event. Teachers could allow the students to demonstrate this capability in various ways—for example, a graphic organizer poster showing causes and effects, a newspaper article, or a podcast of a simulated radio program. Do remember our cautionary note in Module J: although options for students' products and performances may be offered, we would need the *same* criteria for evaluation. In this example, our primary criteria would be *accuracy, completeness*, and *justification* of stated causes and effects.

Of course, feasibility must be considered. Teachers will need to find the practical balance point between individualized assessments and standardized, one-size-fits-all measures. Nonetheless, we believe that classroom assessments can indeed be responsive to students' differences while still providing what is needed—sound evidence and telling information about student learning against common goals.

Finally, we come to Stage 3, where we develop our learning plan to help students achieve the desired results of Stage 1 and equip them for their "performances of understanding" in Stage 2. In Stage 3, differentiated instruction flourishes as we consider variety in the background knowledge, interests, and preferred learning methods of our students. A variety of specific approaches and techniques for responsive teaching are discussed in the following sections. In the meantime, we use the UbD Template to provide a summary of how differentiation fits within the context of backward design (see Figure N.1).

Figure N.1

Backward Design and Differentiation

Stage 1—Desired Results

Established Goals	Transfer
The content standards and other goals do not change; that is, these are what we want all students to attain. (Exception: Students with an authorized IEP pursue the goals specified in their unique plan.)	*Students will be able to independently use their learning to . . .* The long-term transfer goals do not change; that is, these are what we want all students to attain. (Exception: Students with an authorized IEP pursue the goals specified in their unique plan.)

Meaning

UNDERSTANDINGS	ESSENTIAL QUESTIONS
The big ideas of content do not vary. In reality, some students will be able to go into greater depth, but the desired understandings should remain a fixed target for all.	Essential questions should reflect the big ideas that we want all students to come to understand. Because essential questions are open-ended, they allow various entry points, as well as different depths of response.

Acquisition

Students will know . . .	*Students will be skilled at . . .*
	Although knowledge and skills are linked to the goals or content standards, some differentiation may be needed to address knowledge or skill gaps or to extend learning for those students who demonstrate mastery. Pre-assessments are necessary to reveal these needs.

Stage 2—Evidence

Evaluative Criteria	Assessment Evidence
Although students may be given options to show their learning in varied ways, the criteria for evaluating their performance need to remain constant in order for the assessment to be a valid measure of Stage 1 goals.	PERFORMANCE TASK In Stage 2, teachers collect evidence of learning based on the goals of Stage 1. Some differentiation of the assessments may be appropriate. For example, students may be allowed to develop varied products and performances to demonstrate their understanding and proficiency. OTHER EVIDENCE In addition, teachers may allow certain modifications (e.g., allowing oral rather than written responses), as long as acceptable evidence of the targeted learning is obtained.

Stage 3—Learning Plan

Pre- and ongoing assessments are critical to reveal the need for, and nature of, differentiated instruction.

Pre-assessment

Progress Monitoring

Differentiated instruction is appropriate in Stage 3 to address student differences in background knowledge and experience, skill levels, interests, talents, and learning profiles. Designers need to consider ways in which lessons, activities, and resources might be personalized without sacrificing unit goals.

Tailoring the Learning Plan

How will the learning plan reflect the range of abilities, styles, and interests of your students? How will the work be personalized and differentiated in order to achieve the Stage 1 goals (without compromising them)?

A hallmark of good instruction is a learning plan that reflects the typical diversity of students as opposed to one that only suits the strengths and comfort level of the teacher. In even the smallest and most select classes, students have a diversity of background experiences, interests, abilities, and preferred learning styles; in the average classroom the differences are often significant—and typically overwhelming to novice or ill-equipped teachers. Yet it is our professional obligation to design a learning plan in Stage 3 mindful of who the learners are, not who we wish them to be.

Differentiation expert Carol Ann Tomlinson (1999) offers a useful framework for tailoring instruction and assessment where appropriate. She proposes that we can differentiate input (how content is presented and accessed), process (how students work), and products (of student work and assessments). Our decisions are determined by learners' differences in their readiness (background experiences, prior knowledge, skill levels), learning profile (preferred style, culture, gender), and interests. The relationship between these elements can be shown as a grid that suggests the possibilities of the intersection of these variables.

	INPUT	PROCESS	PRODUCT
Readiness			
Learning Profile			
Interests			

An example of tailoring the learning plan via inputs is a social studies unit on colonial America in which the teacher provides different source materials on the topic at various reading levels (textbook, reference books, picture books, videos, web-based resources), and allows students some choice on how they learn the material (e.g., computer simulation, independent reading, cooperative group activity, interactive notebook), as the *X*s on the grid suggest.

	INPUT	PROCESS	PRODUCT
Readiness	X		
Learning Profile	X		
Interests			

Here's an example of tailoring the learning plan via process and products. In a unit involving research and statistics, students are asked to collect, organize, and communicate data on trends for a particular topic to a target audience. As the *Xs* on the grid suggest, students could chose a topic of interest (e.g., sports statistics, fashion trends) to research and then present information in a way that suits their learning preferences and interests (e.g., visual display, quantitative chart, written summary).

	INPUT	PROCESS	PRODUCT
Readiness			
Learning Profile		X	X
Interests		X	X

Alternatively, in speech class we could hold the product constant (e.g., an oral presentation) while allowing choice on process (e.g., topic of the student's choice).

Figures N.2 and N.3 provide many possibilities for tailoring the learning plan to address the diversity of your learners.

Design Tip: Feasibility must be considered when tailoring a unit plan to meet the diverse needs and interests of learners. Because there are typically more options than can realistically be implemented, you are encouraged to choose those variations that are most manageable and likely to have the highest yield for the greatest number of learners based on the desired results stated in Stage 1.

Using the Facets for Differentiation

The six facets of understanding were originally conceived as indicators of understanding for use in assessment (Stage 2), yet they have proven to be a useful frame for developing alternative activities and approaches to learning in Stage 3. You can use the six facets to brainstorm possible learning activities (mindful, of course, of the desired results of Stage 1 and the needed assessment evidence of Stage 2). Here is an example for a middle school unit on the Civil War.

> *Explanation*—Explain the key causes and effects of important events in the Civil War. Compare to other incidents of civil strife.
>
> *Interpretation*—Interpret the war through the main character in *Red Badge of Courage* or the images chosen by Ken Burns in his video series on the war.
>
> *Application*—Debate the legacy of the war in North-South relations today. (Is it over? Has a cold war been going on ever since? Are there

still significant differences in Southern and Northern views of the relation of individuals, states, and the country?)

Perspective—Discuss the war from the perspective of the Northern side, the Southern side, a European, a Native American, a rich landowner, a poor worker.

Empathy—Imagine the experience of a Southern family whose home and farm was destroyed by Sherman's army. Write their journal entries.

Self-Knowledge—Reflect: What do you believe is worth fighting for? Can you imagine your family torn apart by political issues?

Figure N.2

Strategies for Differentiating Input

Consider the various possibilities for differentiating *input* (how you will present and how learners will access content). Check those options that will be effective and feasible for your learning plan.

READINESS

_____ Provide texts at varied reading levels and in students' primary languages.

_____ Provide supplementary materials at varied reading levels.

_____ Provide audiotaped materials.

_____ Use videos to supplement and support explanations and lectures.

_____ Use texts with key portions highlighted.

_____ Provide organizers to guide notetaking.

_____ Provide key vocabulary lists for reference.

_____ Use reading buddies or partners to work with text materials.

_____ Use flexible groupings to address knowledge and skill gaps.

_____ Other: _____

LEARNING PROFILE

_____ Present information orally, visually, and in writing.

_____ Use applications, examples, and illustrations from various intelligences.

_____ Use materials, applications, examples, and illustrations from both genders and a range of cultures and communities.

_____ Use materials that connect content to students' cultures.

_____ Teach from both whole-to-part and part-to-whole approaches.

_____ Demonstrate ideas in addition to talking about them.

_____ Use wait time to allow for student reflection.

_____ Other: _____

INTERESTS

_____ Provide interest centers to encourage further exploration of topics.

_____ Provide a wide range of materials related to student interests and cultures.

_____ Use student questions to guide lectures, materials, and assignments.

_____ Other: _____

One option for using the facets for differentiation is to give students choices (e.g., "Work on two of the listed activities") and then have students "jigsaw" their parts with other students who worked on different activities.

Design Task: Use the six facets worksheet in Figure N.4 to brainstorm ideas for differentiating your learning plan.

Pre-assessments and Formative Assessments

As we noted earlier, these initial ideas about differentiation are somewhat general. They reflect the idea that our class is diverse and provide suggestions for accommodating that diversity. But we need to push further and ask more concrete questions.

Figure N.3

Strategies for Differentiating Process and Product

Consider the various possibilities for differentiating *process* (how learners will make meaning of the content) and *product* (how they will show their learning). Check those options that will be effective and feasible for your learning plan.

Readiness

_____ Use tiered activities (activities at different levels of difficulty, but focused on the same learning goals).

_____ Provide detailed and highly structured task directions for learners who need it, while leaving the task more open for the more capable and independent students.

_____ Provide resource materials at varied levels of readability and sophistication.

_____ Provide teacher-led miniworkshops on needed skills at varied levels of complexity based on student needs.

_____ Provide tailored homework assignments based on readiness.

_____ Provide materials in the primary language of second-language learners.

_____ Other: _____

Learning Profile

_____ Allow multiple options for how students express their learning (varied products and performances to allow learners to work to their strengths).

_____ Balance competitive, collegial, and independent work arrangements.

_____ Allow students to have choices regarding their preferred working mode (e.g., visually, orally, kinesthetically, in writing).

_____ Other: _____

Interests

_____ Establish interest-based work groups and discussion groups.

_____ Use both like-interest and mixed-interest work groups.

_____ Use the jigsaw cooperative strategy to allow students to specialize in aspects of a topic they find interesting.

_____ Allow students to propose interest-based projects and independent studies (related to the content being learned).

_____ Develop activities that seek multiple perspectives on topics and issues.

_____ Other: _____

For example, *Who is in this class* this *year? What do these specific children need? Given where we want them to end up, from what point are they starting? What changes are likely to be required in the learning plan if the desired results are going to be met by this group of individuals?* These questions underscore the vital importance of including pre-assessments and formative assessments into unit designs, especially units to be taught early in the year or that involve completely new content. We need to pre-assess students' current ability levels, needs, and interests if we are to achieve our unit goals, and we need to get feedback throughout the unit if we are to help them attain the Stage 1 goals. In the new UbD Template, we make an explicit and deliberate effort to call designers' attention to this need by adding space for pre-assessment and ongoing formative assessment ideas to the framework of Stage 3.

Figure N.4

Differentiating Using the Six Facets

Use the six facets of understanding to brainstorm ideas for differentiating your learning plan.

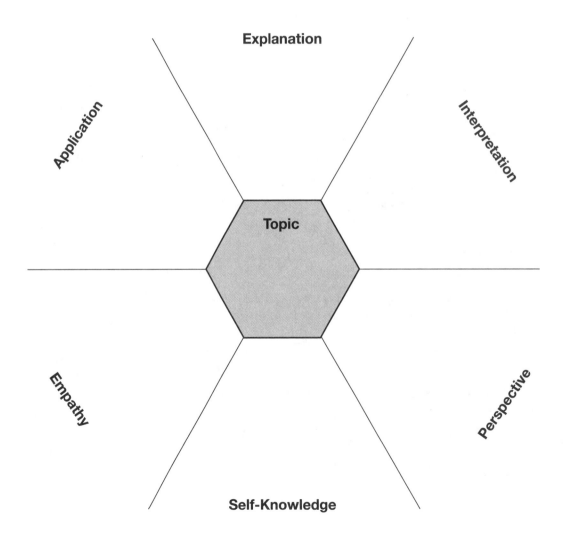

Why is formative assessment in Stage 3 and not Stage 2? Stage 2 asks us to determine the needed *summative* evidence for assessing attainment of the desired results (Stage 1). Although summative assessments often receive the most attention, pre-assessments and formative assessments provide critical "along the way" feedback to guide instruction in response to the nature and needs of the diverse learners. In other words, we are arguing that getting and using feedback during the unit is an instructional move more than an assessment move. Pre-assessments and formative assessments have little to do with formal evaluation or grades of achievement related to Stage 1. Rather, they are part of the learning process—for both teacher and students. Waiting until the end of a unit to find out how well students are learning and how they might learn better is too late. In short, in Stage 3 we consider assessments *for* learning, whereas in Stage 2 we consider assessments *of* learning.

Misconception Alert

A caution about the meaning of "formative assessment" is in order, based on common misuse of this term. An assessment is only formative if it is an interim look at how much progress has been made against a future long-term goal, and if we can therefore use the feedback to adjust in time. (It is "formative" because we can be helped by the feedback going forward; "summative" assessment is over and done with.) Thus asking students to write various papers each month is a formative assessment against the long-term goal of masterful writing. However, a typical midterm test or quiz is rarely a formative assessment because it looks only backward—did you learn what was taught in the previous weeks?—and is thus really summative. This is also clear when we consider the aim of a pre-assessment in which we will use the same test later in the course, perhaps multiple times, to see if adequate progress is being made toward a long-term goal. All genuine formative assessment is about seeing where we are en route so that we know where we stand now against a later goal, and so that we can make adjustments, if needed, in time.

Plan to Adjust

As the discussion thus far suggests, the unit plan is not finished, paradoxically, until there is a *plan to adjust*. A unit will rarely succeed if we only implement it the way we wrote it before finding out who the students are and—especially—how they react to initial instruction and assessment. Learning is most successful when performers get lots of feedback against goals and have opportunities to use that feedback in time. This is as true for teachers as it is for students. Think of the football coach who changes the game plan, based on the unfolding of the game. He typically consults a large laminated card of all possible plays and calls new ones in light of developing game conditions and results. Although teachers always have an urge to stick to the schedule they wrote, it makes little sense to do so if the goal is achievement as opposed to coverage and rigid and arbitrary pacing of content delivery.

Now let's examine each of these types of Stage 3 assessments—pre-assessments and formative assessments—in more detail.

Pre-assessments

Pre-assessments typically precede instruction and are used to check students' prior knowledge and skill levels, and to identify misconceptions, interests, or learning style preferences. Such pre-assessments provide information to assist teacher planning and reveal any differentiated instruction or assessment that may be needed. Examples of such assessments include skill checks, knowledge surveys, interest or learning preference checks, checks for misconceptions, and many other tools. Note: The results of pre-assessments should not count in a student's final grade (even if the work is sometimes marked to note where students stand at the outset).

Here is a set of low-prep, high-yield pre-assessment techniques that provide efficient diagnostic checks of student prior knowledge and misconceptions:

- *K-W-L*—Before introducing a new topic or skill, ask students what they already *k*now (or think they know) about the topic or skill. Record their responses on a board or piece of chart paper in the *K* column. (Sometimes students make statements that are incorrect or reveal misconceptions.) Next, ask them what they *w*ant to know (or *w*hat questions they have) about the topic or skill. Record these responses in the *W* column. (Their questions often reveal interests or "hooks" to the topic. In some cases, their questions reveal misconceptions that will need to be addressed.) As the lesson or unit proceeds, summarize *l*earnings and record them in the *L* column as they occur. (This point provides an opportunity to go back and correct any misconceptions that may have been initially recorded in the *K* column.)
- *Pretest (Nongraded)*—Give students a pretest to check their prior knowledge of key facts and concepts. Use the results to plan instruction and selection of resources. Make sure that students know that the results will not count toward final grades.
- *Skills Check (Nongraded)*—Have students demonstrate their proficiency with a targeted skill or process. It is helpful to have a proficiency checklist or developmental rubric to use in assessing the degree of skill competence. Students can then use the checklist or rubric for ongoing self-assessment.
- *Web/Concept Map*—Ask students to create a web or concept map to show the elements or components of a topic or process. This technique is especially effective in revealing whether students have gaps in their knowledge and the extent to which they understand relationships among the elements.

- *Misconception Check*—Present students with common errors or predictable misconceptions regarding a designated topic, concept, skill, or process. See if they are able to identify the error or misconception and explain why it is erroneous or flawed. The misconception check can also be presented in the form of a true-false quiz in which students must agree or disagree with statements or examples; or a multiple-choice ungraded quiz in which the distractors reflect misconceptions. The Force Concept Inventory in physics is such an assessment, widely used in schools and colleges, administered pre-instruction and post-instruction, to see if common misconceptions are overcome.

Design Task: Use the worksheet in Figure N.5 to identify pre-assessments and possible ways to differentiate your learning plan.

Figure N.5

Using Information from Pre-assessment

Identify one or more pre-assessment techniques to check the readiness levels of students for the identified knowledge and skills in Stage 1. Use the Knowledge and Skills columns to plan possible approaches for meeting the needs of struggling and advanced learners.

Pre-assessments to Check for Readiness	Knowledge	Skills
☐ K-W-L for _____ _____	Ideas for building needed background knowledge or addressing skill gaps for struggling learners	
☐ Pretest on _____ _____		
☐ Skills check for _____ _____		
☐ Web/concept map on _____ _____	Ideas for extending knowledge/skill learning for advanced learners	
☐ Misconception check for _____ _____		

Formative Assessments

Formative assessments occur concurrently with instruction. These ongoing assessments provide information to guide teaching and learning for improving achievement. Formative assessments include both formal and informal methods, such as ungraded quizzes, oral questioning, observations, draft work, prompted think-alouds, student-constructed concept maps, dress rehearsals, peer response groups, and portfolio reviews.

Any successful athletic coach or sponsor of an extracurricular activity (e.g., yearbook, orchestra, debate, or theater) recognizes the value of ongoing assessment and continuous adjustment in achieving maximum performance—and so do the best teachers. Accordingly, we have to "design in" formative assessments and opportunities to act on the feedback if achievement is to be optimized.

Whole-Class Formative Assessments

The following ongoing assessment techniques can be used to obtain a quick check of a whole class or group of students.

- *Hand Signals*—Ask students to display a designated hand signal to indicate their understanding of a designated concept, principle, or process.

  Thumbs up = I understand _____ and can explain it.
  Thumbs down = I do not yet understand _____.
  Wave hand = I'm not completely sure about _____.

- *Responses Using Paddles or Whiteboards*—Have students record a response on a paddle or small whiteboard and hold it up.

  Prediction—*What number should appear next in the sequence?*
  Agree (A) or Disagree (D)—*Does this example belong in this pattern?*

- *Learner Response System*—Use LRSs, or clickers, to have students record a response to a question or a prompt. The results can be tabulated on the teacher's computer to provide immediate feedback on individuals and groups within a class.

- *Misconception Check*—Present students with common or predictable misconceptions about a designated concept, principle, or process. Ask them to agree or disagree. Students can respond using hand signals, whiteboards, LRSs, or on paper.

- *Anonymous Exit Card ("Ticket to Leave")*—Periodically distribute index cards and ask students to complete the cards at the conclusion of a class period, end of the week, or other regular interval. Here are some examples of questions to ask:

  What are the most important things you learned about _____?
  What do you understand about _____?
  What don't you understand yet? What questions do you have?
  Upon collecting the cards, scan them, looking for patterns (e.g., areas where many students have questions).

- *Observations*—Carefully observe students as they work or respond to questions. Observe the work they produce. What areas of strength and weakness do you notice?

Individual Formative Assessments

The following ongoing assessment techniques provide a quick check of the knowledge, skill levels, and degree of understanding of individual students. Of course, oral questioning and observation can be used to provide ongoing assessment of individuals as well.

- *Exit Card ("Ticket to Leave")*—Periodically distribute index cards and ask students to complete the cards at the conclusion of a class period, end of the week, or other regular interval. Students must include their names.

  Example 1: I.Q. Card
  Side 1—Based on our study of (unit topic), list a big idea that you understand in the form of a summary statement.
  Side 2—Identify something about (unit topic) that you do not yet fully understand (as a statement or a question).

  Example 2: 3-2-1 Summary
  List 3 things that you learned about _____ (topic or skill).
  List 2 examples or applications of _____ (topic or skill).
  List 1 question that you have about _____ (topic or skill).

  Example 3: What's Working?
  Side 1—List the things that are helping you learn.
  Side 2—Identify things that have been difficult or are not working for you.

- *Weekly Letter*—Have students write a letter to the teacher and parents summarizing what they have learned during the past week. Students are asked to reflect on their progress during the week and set a learning goal for the upcoming week.
- *Web/Concept Map*—Ask students to create a web or concept map to show the elements or components of a topic or process. This technique reveals if students understand relationships among elements.
- *One-Minute Essay*—Periodically have students complete a brief essay summarizing what they think they understand about a given topic.
- *Question Box/Board*—Establish a location, such as a question box, bulletin board, or e-mail address, where students may post questions about things that they do not understand. (This technique may be preferred by those students who are uncomfortable admitting publicly that they do not understand.)

Design Tip: Readers of this *Guide* may be using learner response systems (clickers) for formative assessment. These are particularly well suited to ongoing feedback that is informative to you without being embarrassing to students because only you need know who gave which answer to a problem. Small whiteboards, answer paddles, or index cards serve as low-tech equivalents of the clickers.

Design Tip: Try to build in at least one day in your unit plan when nothing is planned. Because adjustments are inevitable (based on results of formative assessments), you have to "design in" time to adjust. In other words, the best designs are not overpacked and set in stone but are modifiable and adjusted as needed to cause the desired results. You have to plan to adjust. At the very least, that means not overplanning and then convincing yourself that there is no time to adjust.

Design Tip: Don't consider a unit design to be finished until it has been edited based on pre-assessment results. Set aside time in planning periods to discuss results from diagnostic-type assessments at the beginning of each year, semester, or course; and finish unit design accordingly.

Design Task: Review the suggestions for differentiating instruction and assessment presented in Figures N.2 and N.3, as well as the online assessments listed in the next section. Given your unit goals and your knowledge of your students, mark an *X* next to each suggestion or idea that you believe would support their learning *and* be feasible for you to implement. Then insert the selected ideas into your learning plan.

Further approaches can be found online in Figure N.6, General Ideas for Differentiating Instruction and Assessment; Figure N.7, Ideas for Differentiating Instruction and Assessment for Reading; Figure N.8, Ideas for Differentiating Instruction and Assessment for Writing; Figure N.9, Ideas for Differentiating Instruction and Assessment for Math and Science; and Figure N.10, Ideas for Challenging High Achievers.

Self-Assessment—Review Criteria for Module N

Review your current Stage 3 learning plan against the following self-assessment questions. Revise the learning plan as needed.

- Does the learning plan make clear to students where they're going (the learning goals), why (reason for learning the content), and what is required of them (performance requirements and evaluative criteria)?
- Does the learning plan include one or more hooks to engage learners around the unit's important ideas?
- Does the learning plan provide adequate opportunities for students to explore big ideas and essential questions, and to receive instruction to equip them for the required performance?
- Does the learning plan provide sufficient opportunities for learners to rethink, rehearse, revise, or refine their work based upon timely feedback?
- Does the learning plan include opportunities for students to self-evaluate their work, reflect on their learning, and set future goals?

- Is the learning plan tailored in response to differences in learners' readiness levels, learning profiles, and interests?
- Is the learning plan organized and sequenced for maximum engagement and effectiveness?

Further Information on the Ideas and Issues in This Module

Understanding by Design, 2nd ed. (Wiggins & McTighe, 2005). Chapter 9, pages 218–222. An overview of the "macro" (course planning) and the "micro" (lesson planning) aspects of design, in light of a focus on unit planning.

Understanding by Design: Professional Development Workbook. (McTighe & Wiggins, 2004). Pages 212–227. Worksheets on how to construct, sequence, and self-assess the flow of the unit plan.

Schooling by Design: Mission, Action, and Achievement (Wiggins & McTighe, 2007). Chapter 5, "What's My Job When I Am with Students?" A discussion of how to think about one's obligation as a planner of work and a reviewer of results.

Integrating Differentiated Instruction and Understanding by Design: Connecting Content and Kids. (Tomlinson & McTighe, 2006). Offers greater detail on how to integrate understanding by design and differentiation.

Guide for Instructional Leaders, Guide 2: An ASCD Action Tool (Wiggins, Brown, & O'Connor, 2003). Pages 1–22. A constructed dialogue about how to think through the design of curriculum, mindful of learning goals.

References

McTighe, J., & Wiggins, G. (2004). *Understanding by Design: Professional development workbook.* Alexandria, VA: ASCD.

Tomlinson, C. (1999). *The differentiated classroom: Responding to the needs of all learners.* Alexandria, VA: ASCD.

Tomlinson, C., & McTighe, J. (2006). *Integrating differentiated instruction and Understanding by Design: Connecting content and kids.* Alexandria, VA: ASCD.

Wiggins, G., Brown, J. L., & O'Connor, K. (2003). *Guide for instructional leaders, Guide 2: An ASCD Action Tool.* Alexandria, VA: ASCD.

Wiggins, G., & McTighe, J. (2005). *Understanding by Design* (2nd ed.). Alexandria, VA: ASCD.

Wiggins, G., & McTighe, J. (2007). *Schooling by design: Mission, action, and achievement.* Alexandria, VA: ASCD.

Module O

···························

Designing the Lesson Plan
for Your Unit

···

Purpose: To develop lesson plans by sequencing for optimal learning and coding for alignment.

Desired Results:

Unit designers will understand that

- The best lesson plans are planned backward from clear and worthy course and unit goals.
- Effective lessons carefully sequence the learning events for optimal engagement and effectiveness—and such a sequence is typically different from the layout of the textbook.
- The textbook is a resource in support of designated goals, not the course syllabus or sole resource for lessons.
- Effective lessons are tightly aligned to desired results (Stage 1) and assessment evidence (Stage 2).

Unit designers will be able to

- Choose from various unit-sequencing options for their learning plan.
- Develop lesson plans for their unit that reflect T-M-A and WHERETO elements based on unit goals and the needs of their students.
- Select an appropriate lesson plan format if one is not already prescribed.

Module Design Goals: In this module, you will refine your Stage 3 learning plan by considering four unit-sequencing options for lessons and learning events. You will also have the opportunity to code your learning events against T-M-A or WHERETO elements.

You should work on Module O if you wish to flesh out specific lesson plans for Stage 3 or you want to think through the optimal sequence for the unit elements.

You might skim or skip Module O if you do not need or want detailed lesson plans.

···

Throughout this *Guide* we have been coaching you on how to develop a unit of study. And although no hard and fast rules exist for how to define "unit" in education, the most common meaning is that a unit is *an integrated set of lessons, framed around a unifying goal or idea*. Up to this point, we have referred to Stage 3 in a unit in terms of a general learning plan, and the examples we have shown provide primarily a summary or listing of key learning events. In this module, we examine more detailed lesson plans and their role in directing the day-to-day actions in the classroom.

Lesson Plans in UbD

A focus on lesson planning raises a few important questions:

- What exactly should be included in a lesson plan, and how does it differ, if at all, from a UbD unit plan?
- How is backward design applied at the lesson level?
- How much detail should lesson plans contain?
- How should the lessons and learning events in a unit be sequenced to be most engaging and effective?
- What is the role of textbooks and related resources in lesson planning?
- How about pacing guides?

Backward Design and Lesson Planning

We'll examine these questions by considering an analogy with popular mapping applications like MapQuest or Google Maps. Online maps include a zooming tool to allow users to get a wide-angled view of an entire region and then progressively zoom downward, all the way to individual streets and buildings. We can view curriculum similarly, from a big-picture vantage point down to its smallest unit:

- A *curriculum* is organized to reflect mission (e.g., critical thinking) and program goals (e.g., scientific inquiry).
- These long-term goals are framed by *subjects* (e.g., science) and courses (e.g., biology).
- *Courses* are composed of units (e.g., the cell).
- *Units* are composed of lessons (e.g., plant cells).
- *Lessons* are composed of events (e.g., viewing a plant cell through a microscope).
- *Events* are composed of step-by-step actions and directions (e.g., procedures for focusing the scope and recording observations).

Just as travelers need to know their overall destination before embarking on the trip, events and daily lessons need to be planned backward from course and unit goals, mindful of the larger mission and program outcomes. Developed in this way, lessons are more likely to provide engaging, coherent, and helpful scaffolding toward a significant learning target, just as online maps and GPS devices allow drivers to follow an efficient and effective route to their end point. Failure to plan lessons backward increases the likelihood that lessons will consist of directionless activities or coverage of discrete content objectives without a clear, worthy, and unifying end in mind. To shift the metaphor, a collection of individual events does not ensure a coherent lesson, unit, or course over time, any more than a pile of bricks automatically results in a solid and aesthetically pleasing building. There has to be a detailed blueprint of the whole to ensure that each part belongs; and there has to be an intelligent plan and scope of work by the general contractor to ensure that the whole is achieved in the most efficient and logical sequence.

Essential Lesson Elements

So, if we plan lessons backward from broader goals, what should these daily plans include? Some educators who have become acquainted with Understanding by Design assume that the three-stage unit-planning template can also serve as the organizing format for individual lessons. We do *not* recommend this. The key elements of UbD—understandings, essential questions, and transfer performances—are too complex and multifaceted to be satisfactorily addressed within a single lesson—and are sometimes too complex to be satisfactorily addressed within a single unit. Moreover, essential questions and transfer goals should be revisited over time, not put to rest by the end of a single class period.

Having clearly defined the key elements of a UbD unit, what, then, should be in a lesson plan? The phrase *lesson plan* is ambiguous. It can refer to a plan we develop from scratch for our own sake in managing instruction, and it can refer to an outline of previously planned work we provide primarily for the sake of supervisory oversight. In UbD, the phrase is ambiguous in another important way. Unless we know how specific Stage 3 in the original unit plan is, and unless we know how much freedom a teacher has as a designer of lessons, we don't really know what kind of a plan is called for—either for ourselves or for supervisors. At one extreme, where schools require teachers to work from an official curriculum, a lesson plan might simply involve a relatively straightforward task of making a personal calendar that parcels out the planned events. (This is arguably what happens now in textbook-driven or programmed instruction.) On the other hand, if the original Stage 3 is very broad, then teachers will have to flesh out more detailed lesson plans for day-to-day instruction. Such lessons will need to closely align with Stages 1 and 2 and include the essential elements previously discussed.

Nonetheless, we believe that any effective lesson plan includes several basic components, regardless of particular local needs, emphases, and interests. Effective lesson plans include a meaningful objective, appropriate events, formative assessments, a plan to adjust, and appropriate closure.

- *Meaningful Objective*—An objective for the lesson is proposed, justified in terms of past learning and student interest, and linked to longer-term goals (that is, aligned with specific unit elements of Stages 1 and 2, to course and program goals, and to mission)—the *W* in WHERETO.
- *Appropriate Events*—Learning events are created to maximize engaged and effective learning, mindful of student diversity, in terms of the unit goals and goal types (transfer, meaning, or acquisition [T-M-A]).
- *Formative Assessments*—Ongoing assessments and "look-fors" enable teachers to check along the way for learners' misconceptions or skill deficits, and adjust their instruction accordingly.
- *A Plan to Adjust*—When formative assessments reveal learning difficulties, it does not make sense to ignore them and continue marching through the curriculum. Learning plans need to build in time for teachers to respond to inevitable student challenges and unpredicted student interests and responses as the work of the day unfolds.
- *Appropriate Closure*—Effective lesson plans typically conclude with a lesson summary or debrief, links to past and future lessons, and student self-assessment or reflection.

Lesson Plan Formats

It wouldn't be wise for us to argue for one official template for lesson plans in UbD, because many schools and districts already have an agreed-upon format that teachers are expected to use. Regardless of the particular elements or format that a teacher, school, or district chooses to include in a lesson, keep in mind that UbD was developed in part to overcome a bad habit in lesson planning—losing sight of long-term aims and focusing only on a plan for each day or, at most, a week. The danger in the traditional approach is that learning outcomes can become divided up into very small bits of content in ways that make it less likely that learners will make the intellectual connections and develop the complex performance abilities that lie at the heart of meaning-making and transfer. Thus it is vital to ensure that any formal lesson plans and their associated formats signal that lessons are transparently built backward from unit goals and are deliberate in signaling the need to build in meaning-making and transfer activities that work together across lessons.

Coding Lesson Events

A practical way of ensuring this coherence and alignment is through the use of a simple coding system. In this regard, we strongly recommend that before you become too invested in (or bogged down by) detailed lesson planning, you first simply summarize the key learning events in sequence for your Stage 3 learning plan. Then code these events to the desired results of Stage 1 and associated assessments in Stage 2.

In addition to basic coding for alignment with Stages 1 and 2, designers can also code their lessons using other schema, such as T-M-A, WHERETO, Bloom's taxonomy categories, or Webb's Depth of Knowledge.

⊃ **Design Task:** Using one (or more) of the coding schemes, code the learning events in your unit. Is there proper alignment with Stages 1 and 2? Is anything missing (e.g., meaning-making activities or the opportunity for learners to act on feedback)?

Another reason we hesitate to offer a fixed lesson plan template is that lesson types and timing differ. For example, in the opening lesson or lessons for a new unit, teachers preview the topic and help learners see the purpose and relevance of the targeted learning. Such lessons include some diagnostic (or pre-) assessment to check for prior knowledge and skills, misconceptions, and students' interests related to the topic. We also recommend that teachers begin with some stimulating hook to engage learners early on. These ideas reflect the *W* and the *H* in WHERETO.

Of course, we do not need a new hook or pre-assessment for every lesson within the unit. However, these unique lesson elements are arguably crucial at the start.

At the conclusion of a unit, the culminating lesson or lessons typically include a unit summary; student self-assessments, reflection, and goal setting; a consideration of "so what?" (that is, making connections to future learning and real-world applications); and a preview of the next unit. Once again, not every lesson within a unit will need these particular elements, but they are important for closure.

Figure O.1 summarizes the distinctive qualities of the beginning and ending lessons, coded for the WHERE elements.

Considering Audience and Purpose in Lesson Planning

Another relevant question has to do with the degree of detail that a lesson plan should include. In other words, when are step-by-step directions needed, and when is it OK to simply summarize the key learning events?

To explore the variable of lesson detail, consider this example of a single learning event, a portion of a lesson in algebra:

Mission: Problem solving, critical thinking
Subject: Mathematics
Course: Algebra I
Unit: Order of Operations and Properties
Lesson: Why do we need an order of operations?
Event: *Make Up Your Own Rules* (the first of five events)

In this learning event, students will review the notion of rules and properties, and see how to differentiate between the two. Students should experience the need for order of operations while seeing the logic to having core properties. Often students

Figure O.1

Beginning and Ending Lessons

Beginning Lessons in a Unit Include	Ending Lessons in a Unit Include
• An introduction to the unit goals and the purpose/value of learning them (W). • A preview of the evidence needed to demonstrate learning, including the transfer performance tasks (W). • A preview of the rubrics to be used, along with models/exemplars of effective performance (W). • A review of the unit sequence (W). • Pre-assessment to check for student readiness—knowledge, skill levels, potential misconceptions, and interests related to the unit topic (W). • A hook to engage interest and focus learning (H). Note: *There is not a prescribed sequence for these beginning elements. For example, a teacher may begin a new unit with a hook, and then introduce the unit goals. Alternatively, a teacher might start by showing models of excellent performance, and then describe the unit goals and assessments.*	• A return to the essential questions to consider what has been learned and better understood (E-2, R). • An opportunity for students to self-assess their performance based on the unit goals and assessment results. • A reflection on the "so what"; for example, *What can I now do with what I have learned? How will this learning help me in school? In my life?* (E-2, R). • An opportunity for students to set future learning goals (E-2). • A preview of the next unit (W) and its connection to the one just completed. Note: *The end of the unit affords the opportunity for teachers to reflect on the unit's effectiveness, self-assess their own teaching, and identify adjustments they plan to make when teaching the unit in the future.*

are given properties and conventions, told to memorize them, and then drilled on their use. Such acquisition-oriented lessons rarely engage learners deeply or result in deep understanding of the targeted content. Here is an alternate approach designed to help students "make meaning" or come to understand the difference between properties and conventions:

> Tell students that you have declared the next 20 minutes to be "Make Up Rules" time. You're going to suspend past rules—*every reasonable answer is a right answer*. (The goal is to get more than one answer each time.) Do one simple example together to get started: $5 - 3 \times 2$. Other than the correct answer of -1, you can get 1 if you change the order of operations *and* the numbers for subtraction, or 4 if you work from left to right *without* applying order of operations.

Give students a list of problems to play with, using instances that will lead to discussion of the main properties (commutative, associative, and distributive) as well as order of operations. It's fun to have some examples with many possible answers due to order of operations issues; but also include some simple examples, like $5 + 3 + 4$ and $5 - 3 - 4$, to illustrate properties and when they are true. To be sure that students understand, have them try one short example of each (a property and an order-of-operations example with multiple possible "answers") and discuss them before giving a full list of examples.

Lead a discussion of possible answers for each example. For a more complex example of order of operations, recognize the pair or small group that has produced the greatest number of possible answers, and allow them to demonstrate how they got those answers. Have various students explain how they came up with alternate answers for each problem, and then discuss which answer is generally considered "correct."

Use the simpler examples to discuss properties. Students should have a hard time coming up with multiple answers to 4 × 8, but should come up with two answers for 3÷5 by reversing order. Use this to discuss the *idea* of a property, a special characteristic of multiplication that division doesn't have—the ability to reverse order without changing the answer. Discuss the question: *Why would we want this to be true?* At this point, don't worry about labeling it the commutative property.

As students describe how they got their answers, pose the question: *Why is that approach OK? Why is it not OK? Couldn't we all agree to add before we multiply—or work from right to left?* Slowly introduce the possibility that some of the things they learn in math are *not* natural truths but agreed-upon human conventions.

Tell students that "Make Up Rules" time is over; now it's time to come to agreement on what seemingly true properties exist, and what (arbitrary) conventions we need so that we will all interpret the language of mathematics the same way.

Note that this particular "event" is made up of six distinct activities, with fairly detailed directions provided for the teacher. Note also that this event is only a part of an overall lesson containing several such events of varying numbers of activities. Does this example mean to suggest that all lessons in a UbD unit need to be this detailed? Well, it depends on the answer to the essential question for the writing process: for whom and for what purpose is the unit being written? Here are options regarding the level of detail needed in lesson plans:

- *When individual teachers design units for themselves*, they determine the level of detail they need in Stage 3.
- *When curriculum teams or mentors design units for other teachers to use:*
    - Option 1—they provide an outline of major learning events in sequence, and the teachers can flesh out more detailed and personalized lesson plans.
    - Option 2—they provide the detailed lesson plans for teachers to follow.

When writing lesson plans that other educators will be expected to implement (Option 2), the demands for specificity are typically far greater than if a teacher is merely reminding herself of key events and sequence in her own lesson. It is thus conceivable that within the same school district, the lesson plan specifications for writing district curriculum might be quite different from a plan developed for an individual teacher's personal use.

Context may also affect the answer. A new teacher on probation, whose lessons are routinely inspected by supervisors, might be expected to provide much more detail than would an accomplished veteran. And if teacher lesson plans are accessible by parents via online systems, the demands related to audience and purpose may yield a different answer.

Two Cautions

We offer two cautions to school and district administrators regarding lesson plan requirements. First, when teachers are expected to plan their own lessons (rather than implementing previously developed lessons from the district), be sensitive to the hardship of overly detailed lesson formats. We have seen multipage forms for daily plans that require teachers to provide written details on numerous elements (e.g., anticipatory set; daily objective; a "hook"; content standards/benchmarks/ objectives to be learned; focus questions; key vocabulary terms; thinking skills; habits of mind; research-based teaching strategies to be used; learning activities related to various learning modalities or multiple intelligences; pre-assessments; formative assessments; differentiation plans for content, process, and product; ELL and SPED modifications; enrichment for advanced learners; summative assessments; closure activities; homework; preview of tomorrow's lesson; and the teacher's reflection on the lesson). Although well intentioned, such lesson requirements prove to be excessively demanding for most secondary teachers with three to five daily preps or elementary teachers who teach multiple subjects every day.

Second, when detailed curriculum is mandated for teachers by the district, school, or department, we recommend that some flexibility and teacher input be allowed. *It is our view that no curriculum or lesson plan should be "teacher-proof."* Indeed, professional judgment and instructional responsiveness to the needs of learners may be sacrificed if we simply distribute scripted lessons to teachers. Accordingly, we recommend that the final lesson plan be fleshed out (or adapted) by the teacher who will be teaching the unit—when such a lesson plan is needed or desired. The two important caveats, of course, are (1) that any final lesson plan must still meet the key design standards for Stage 3, namely that the plan is likely to engage all students and contribute to the attainment of unit goals; and (2) novice and probationary teachers may need to stick to pre-approved lesson plans until they demonstrate competence with the content and associated pedagogy.

The Role of the Textbook

Throughout the world, instruction in many classrooms consists of simply following the chronology of textbooks. In such cases, lesson planning is ceded to textbook companies. As common and tempting as it is to believe that your teaching sequence must reflect the pagination of the textbook, a moment's thought about the key UbD elements of backward design, essential questions, and transfer tasks should reveal otherwise. By definition, essential questions recur, whereas most textbooks only organize content in an orderly way, like a cookbook or a software manual. Just as it would be foolish to learn English by reading the dictionary page by page, it is unwise to organize learning for understanding by the way the resources are ordered for easy access. The role of the textbook in transfer is similar. We do not learn to drive a car, play a musical instrument, or use software by just reading chapters in which the content is logically organized. We read chapters when the information is needed to help us accomplish a desired performance and solve emergent problems. In other words, the content in the textbook or manual is a *means* to a larger performance end. Backward design reminds us to always keep that end in mind and to teach accordingly.

Why, then, are most textbooks organized the way they are? Like dictionaries and encyclopedias, if you want to find something in a book, it is much easier if the content is organized using a simple topic-related framework. But it does not follow that what is useful for looking things up in a book is the best way to parcel out learning and cause engagement and understanding. In other words, don't confuse the logic of the content organization in a book with the best logic for learning to use content. They are not the same.

Throughout this *Guide*, we have maintained that Stage 3 learning events, instruction, and associated resources (such as textbooks) should be selected and used with the larger learning outcomes and associated assessments in mind. Accordingly, instructional resources, including textbooks and software, should be selected and used because they assist teachers and students in reaching important learning goals. So, try to first lay out the most intelligent syllabus based on your unit or course goals *without* looking at the textbook's table of contents. After thinking through the logic of the learning needed to perform with content (that is, to transfer), then select the relevant textbook chapters and the appropriate sequence.

We suggest that you ask these questions when considering the use of a textbook in your teaching:

- What are the textbook's strengths? Which portions of the book will help students achieve the units' desired results?
- What are the textbook's weaknesses relative to the short- and long-term learning goals? (Most textbook assessments test acquisition goals only. They do not generally offer complex tasks that assess meaning and transfer.)
- What is the best sequence for referencing the book? (Beginning a unit by opening the book to the next chapter may not be the optimal starting place.)

The *O* in WHERETO: *Organize* for Learning and Engagement

Sequence matters! The organization of the learning events can influence their effectiveness and also influence student engagement. Much of schooling is needlessly boring or confusing—not because the content is inherently uninteresting, but because the typical sequence of lessons found in conventional lesson plans and (especially) in typical textbooks involves simply marching through "stuff" with little sense from the outset about the value of the "stuff" and how it fits together in the end. As noted, most commercial textbooks are organized in a linear topic-by-topic manner that undercuts the spiraling and revisiting needed to cause thoughtful, deep, and connective insight.

Whether or not you are a stickler for detail in planning—and even if you are not required to produce written lesson plans—we highly recommend that you develop a thoughtfully sequenced plan of learning events for your unit. Why? Because the right flow of learning activities greatly influences the engagement of learners as well as their ability to make meaning of and transfer the content. In other words, teachers need to think carefully about the O in WHERETO—that is, the organization of the unit.

When units are intended to develop meaning-making and transfer, the learning sequence should not simply consist of a linear march through content. The development of students' understanding develops over time through multiple opportunities to consider (and reconsider) the key ideas of the unit. Similarly, the capacity to transfer learning to new situations typically requires practice, feedback, and revision over time—*not* a one-shot attempt. (The *R* in WHERETO serves as a reminder of these vital points.) In other words, the deepening of understanding and the fluency of transfer is always iterative. You reconsider prior ideas in light of new ideas. You weave in new skills with old skills in confronting the same complex challenges. In short, the best units never just plow through subject matter, but orchestrate a spiraling that allow a revisiting of big ideas and work toward transfer goals.

Alternative Approaches to Sequence

How, then, should we think about the sequence of our learning plan if engagement, understanding, and transfer are valued outcomes? How else might we organize our lessons, and learning events within them, other than following the chronology of a textbook? We suggest these general alternatives to a content-covering sequence:

- *Problem-based learning* and the *case method* as applied in law, business, and medicine
- The *immersion approach* to language learning
- The *narrative structure* as used in literature and film
- The *whole-part-whole approach* applied in athletics and the arts

In the first organizational approach, learning is developed as a result of attempting to solve complex problems, exploring real issues, or analyzing bona fide cases. The requisite knowledge and skills are developed in the context of meaningful application. (Remember our contention that understanding must be earned!)

In the case of learning a new language, students are immersed in a natural language environment within which they must learn to communicate, first by listening and speaking; later through reading and writing. Once again, the basics (vocabulary, grammar rules) are acquired in the context of authentic communication.

The third approach employs a sequence based on narrative structure. The best stories rarely lay out all key facts, biographies, definitions, or themes in the beginning. Instead, they begin *in media res*—we're plunked right in the middle of things, and later the details unfold and begin to make sense. This is the structure of memorable novels, movies, and even the better newspaper and magazine articles.

The fourth approach is the norm in athletics and the arts. The learner knows the desired performance from the start—the soccer game, the painting, or the musical to be performed. All practice and preparation are then transparently linked back to the game, the entire painting, or the play. The particular skills and strategies needed for effective performance (the "pieces") are learned and practiced with constant feedback with the "whole" in mind. This is not a brick-by-brick approach to constructing knowledge. Rather, it is backward design from masterful performance approach to learning. These four varied approaches to instructional sequence may give you ideas for a more engaging, and ultimately successful, learning plan. To further explore sequencing options for your unit, refer to Figure O.2, Analyzing Sequence.

We are well aware that these ideas about sequence, although not new or radical, represent a big shift in habits for most teachers—particularly in light of the widespread use of textbooks. We hope, however, that this module will cause you to experiment with sequence and help you see that other approaches to sequence may better help you achieve your goals than the one you are most comfortable with.

How to Pace and How Not to Pace Lessons

Whether or not you are obligated to a "pacing guide" established by your school or district, we need to make some brief comments about what is appropriate and inappropriate pacing in one's work as a teacher. The point of a pacing guide is to ensure that in the short term you track how you are doing against long-term goals, so that you are on pace to end with the best possible result. Note, however, that in sports the pace refers to the *output*, not the content: are you on pace to produce the best possible performance—that is, in the end, the lowest possible time? Too many teacher pacing guides propose arbitrary paces with arbitrary dates by which content should be covered, as opposed to dates by which content

Figure O.2

Analyzing Sequence: Example and Worksheet

Sequencing Questions	Example (Statistics Unit)	Ideas for Sequencing Your Unit
How will learners be hooked from the start?	• The unit begins with an interesting and accessible problem, not passive learning of new content with no context. • The focus on the question of fairness as the underlying issue is engaging.	
How will learners be made aware of the big picture (and reason for learning the content) all along the way?	• The final performance goal—a "fair" grading system and reflection on the essential question—is known early and constantly referred to in the unit.	
How will the learning unfold in a natural flow, from the learner's point of view?	• The discussions and inquiries from one problem or issue feed back into the original problem. • The textbook material on mean, median, and mode is only introduced when students are ready for it as a potential source of help, given the issues.	

should be *understood in order for ultimate high-level performance to occur*. Don't confuse coverage with learning. You may have to routinely slow down the teaching to increase the learning. Don't confuse pace with arbitrary calendars. In sports, you find the best pace for a runner or a swimmer in part based on that athlete's style and in part by the demands of the race. And sometimes a pace that is slow in the beginning yields a better result in the end than a too-fast start—whether in algebra or the 400-meter race.

Most important, don't hesitate in your lesson planning to build in adjustment days or lessons, based on informal or formal assessments as part of the plan to achieve your goals. Paradoxically, far too many teachers overteach and overplan their daily, weekly, and yearly lessons, making it unlikely that all students will get the feedback and advice they need to best achieve the desired results in the end. After all, the whole point of "split times" in sports is to provide the learner with valuable feedback and timely chances to adjust based on the feedback.

Design Task: Now it is time to apply the ideas of lesson sequence and coding to your unit.

Self-Assessment—Review Criteria for Module O

Use the following questions to self-assess your current unit:

- Are the key events proposed in Stage 3 likely to cause engagement and understanding?
- Is the sequence of events optimal for initial and sustained engagement?
- Is the sequence (and spiraling) of events optimal for causing deepening understanding?
- If there is a deliberate UbD-based approach to lesson planning called for, does the approach keep long-term goals in constant view and avoid arbitrary requirements?

Online you'll find worksheets to help you with your lesson plans and other ideas explored in this module: Figure O.3, Lesson Plan Format; Figure O.4, Alternate Lesson Plan Format; Figure O.5, Example of Lesson Plan Coding Using T-M-A (Algebra); Figure O.6, Lesson Plan Coding Using WHERETO; Figure O.7, Using the Textbook Wisely; and Figure O.8, Sequence Options.

Further Information on the Ideas and Issues in This Module

Schooling by Design: Mission, Action, and Achievement. (Wiggins & McTighe, 2007). Chapter 5 "What Is the Teacher's Job When Teaching?" offers greater depth in an overall approach to planning of instruction.

Understanding by Design, 2nd ed. (Wiggins & McTighe, 2005). Chapter 9, "Planning for Learning," is a comprehensive summary of how to think about Stage 3, honor the ideas of WHERETO, and consider unit planning.

Understanding by Design Professional Development Workbook (McTighe & Wiggins, 2004). Refer to "Stage 3—Learning Plan: Design Tools and Samples" (pp. 21–238) for additional worksheets and design tools related to unit and lesson planning.

Module P

Obtaining and Using Feedback

Purpose: To improve unit design through feedback (Stages 4, 5, 6).

Desired Results:

Unit designers and school administrators will understand that

- A draft unit can be refined as a result of feedback from various sources—from peers, experts, and students, through observation of the unit in action, and via analysis of results (students' performance).

- Design standards provide specific and helpful criteria to guide self-assessment and peer review of UbD units.

- Observable indicators (classroom "look-fors") guide observations during unit implementation and contribute to the unit's effectiveness.

- Following structured protocols will enhance a group's effectiveness during peer review and examination of results (students' performance).

Unit designers, colleagues, and school administrators will be able to

- Refine their draft unit through feedback from self-assessment, peer reviews, implementation, and examination of results.

- Give feedback to others based on design standards, observable classroom indicators, and examination of results.

Module Design Goals: In this module, you will learn various ways to obtain feedback to improve the design and implementation of your unit. You will also learn protocols for analyzing results and getting feedback from students.

You should work on Module P if you have completed your draft unit but have not yet developed a plan to obtain feedback on your design (e.g., via self-assessment, peer and/or expert reviews, observers, students).

You should work on Module P if you are not yet ready to develop a plan to obtain feedback.

You might skim or skip Module P if you and your colleagues already have and use a protocol for gaining feedback on your design work.

Designing UbD units is a demanding endeavor, and few teachers or curriculum designers develop a perfect unit on their first attempt. However, by seeking and acting on feedback, anyone can greatly improve the quality of unit designs. Indeed, the research could not be clearer: feedback is the vehicle for improving performance in any field—including students, athletes, artists, and teacher-designers. In this module we discuss various sources of feedback to use in refining your unit plan. We will also present a full look at UbD design standards, along with structured protocols for peer review and examination of results.

The Unit Design Cycle

By working through this *Guide*, you should now have a solid draft of a unit plan. But you're not done. Unit design should be viewed as an extended and cyclical process of continuous improvement, involving drafting and refinement based on feedback from reviews, implementation, and results.

Once a unit is drafted using the first three stages of backward design, we find it helpful to think of the feedback loop as also having three distinct stages:

Stage 4—The draft unit is reviewed against UbD design standards by

- the designer (self-assessment); and, if possible,
- colleagues (peer review); and perhaps,
- outside experts.

Stage 5—As the unit is implemented with students, feedback comes from

- the teacher's direct observation as to what is and isn't working as the unit unfolds, including information from formative assessments and informal feedback from students; and
- observations from colleagues and administrators using a set of observable indicators (look-fors).

Stage 6—Once the unit has been completed, feedback comes from

- the results from the summative assessments in Stage 2; and
- what worked and what didn't from the students' (and observers') perspectives, and what advice they might have about how to improve the unit.

Figure P.1 is a graphic representation of Stages 4, 5, and 6. The table in Figure P.2 provides a summary of the various feedback opportunities that may be used to guide needed improvements to a unit.

Note: Although it is unlikely that every option will be used for every UbD unit, we do recommend that some feedback be sought from each stage.

We now examine Stages 4, 5, and 6 in greater detail.

Figure P.1

Unit Design and Feedback Loop

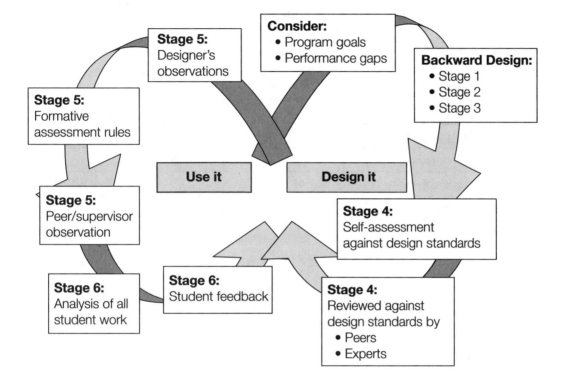

Stage 4: Self-Assessment Against Design Standards

Throughout the *Design Guide*, we have encouraged you to self-assess your emerging unit by considering the review questions provided at the end of each module. Now we recommend a more formal self-assessment of the entire draft once it is finished. We have found that a thorough self-assessment after drafting and before implementation invariably reveals needed edits and refinements. Unit design is like any kind of writing; when you are in the middle of it you can lack perspective, but with a little bit of distance, you can usually spot flaws or oversights.

Design Tip: We suggest that you read through your unit from two perspectives:

- A teacher who might be interested in using the design; for example, *Is the unit plan clear? Is it complete? Could the teacher follow the plan as you intended?*
- A student; for example, *Are the essential questions interesting? Are task directions clear? Will students know what is expected? Are the learning events likely to engage students?*

As you know, we have developed a set of design standards for reviewing UbD units. The design standards have a dual purpose: (1) to guide self-assessment and peer reviews to identify design strengths and needed improvements, and (2) to provide a mechanism for quality control and a means of validating curricular designs.

Figure P.2

UbD Feedback Matrix

Stage	Feedback Source	Drafting	Implementation	Results
4	Self-Assessment	X		
4	Peer/Expert Review	X		
4	Expert Review	X		
5	Designer's Observation		X	X
5	Formative Assessments		X	
5	Outside Observers		X	
6	Analysis of Results			X
6	Students		X	X

The UbD Design Standards 2.0 are listed in Figure P.3, in rubric form. A more detailed version in the form of elaborated rubrics is available online.

Design Task: Review your full draft unit using the design standards in Figure P.3 and make any revisions that are needed.

Stage 4: Peer Review

Despite our hard work and best intentions, we can sometimes get too close to our unit design and have a hard time seeing its weaknesses. Accordingly, we strongly recommend that teachers participate in structured as well as informal peer reviews of their UbD designs, guided by the design standards.

The primary purpose of peer review is to provide feedback to designers for the purpose of helping them improve their designs. However, there are residual benefits. Participants in peer review sessions regularly comment that they get ideas for improving their own unit designs as a result of reviewing the work of colleagues. In addition to the value of the process, the quality of the products is enhanced when teachers are able to refine their unit designs based on feedback and suggestions for improvement.

The UbD peer review process follows a structured protocol to maximize helpful feedback and guidance. A facilitator should review the protocol and the ground rules before each session. It is helpful to hold practice peer review sessions using sample units (we provide some online) before initiating the process with the actual designs of teachers. The skills of giving and receiving feedback need to be modeled and practiced; the fishbowl process is one effective technique that can be used.

The peer review process is well suited for a team or department meeting or a professional development day. Participating teachers should bring copies of their

Figure P.3

UbD Design Standards 2.0

3 = Meets the standard   2 = Partially meets the standard   1 = Does not yet meet the standard

Unit Plan				
Stage 1	**3**	**2**	**1**	**Feedback and Guidance**
1. Specifies the desired long-term transfer goals that involve genuine accomplishment.				
2. Identifies important, transferable ideas worth exploring and understanding.				
3. Identifies understandings stated as full-sentence generalizations: *Students will understand that . . .*				
4. Is framed by a few open-ended, thought-provoking, and focusing essential questions.				
5. Identifies relevant standards, mission, or program goals, to be addressed in all three stages.				
6. Identifies knowledge and skill needed to achieve understanding and address the established goals.				
7. Aligns all the elements so that Stage 1 is focused and coherent.				
Stage 2				
8. Specifies valid assessment evidence of all desired results: Stage 2 aligns with Stage 1.				
9. Includes authentic performance tasks based on one or more facets of understanding.				
10. Provides sufficient opportunities for students to reveal their achievement.				
11. Includes evaluative criteria to align each task to desired results and to provide suitable feedback on performance.				
Stage 3				

12. Includes learning events and instruction needed to help learners a.
   a. Acquire targeted knowledge and skills.
   b. Make meaning of important ideas. b.
   c. Transfer their learning to new situations.
           c.				

13. Effectively incorporates the WHERETO elements so that the unit is likely to be engaging and effective for all learners.				
Overall				
14. Is coherent, with all three stages in alignment.				
15. Is likely to work; is feasible and appropriate for this situation.				

unit designs to be reviewed. Alternately, people can work virtually if designs are accessible online (e.g., through the ubdexchange.org or a school or district server).

Peer Review Protocol

Step 1—*Review of unit designs without designer present*

1. Designer provides a brief overview of the unit and states any issues he or she wishes to have highlighted in the feedback session. Then the designer temporarily leaves the review group.

2. Reviewers first review and discuss the unit design criteria from the design standards (Figure P.3) or specific tests following each stage of backward design.

3. Reviewers silently read the unit and review materials (template, rubrics, handouts, and so on).

4. Each reviewer silently assesses strengths of design first, then weaknesses (in relation to the specific design criteria, not reviewer tastes).

5. Each reviewer jots down notes on an individual review form (available in the downloadable forms online), summarizing the design's strengths and weaknesses before discussing the unit with the review group. Individual reviewers may also note questions that have arisen, whether about some uncertainties they have about the unit plan or, more generally, questions about design issues that might be brought to the faculty as a whole for later discussion.

6. Review group discusses individual reactions.

7. Review group fills out a group version of the review form (available online), summarizing the group's key feedback and guidance. The reviewers rate the unit, if appropriate, using the one-page sheet of design standards (Figure P.3).

Step 2—*Peer discussion of review with designer*

1. Establish roles (e.g., time-keeper and facilitator) and set specific time frame for group feedback and guidance. The facilitator's key job is to gently but firmly ensure that the designer listens (instead of defending).

2. Designer clarifies any technical or logistical issues in response to questions about the unit that arose in Step 1, Item 5, only as requested (without elaborating on rationale or justifying the intent, history, or reasons for choices); the design must stand by itself as much as possible.

3. Reviewers give feedback first, making clear the basis for the comments on the match (or mismatch) among targeted achievements, assessments, and design of learning and teaching, in reference to the design standards. Couching feedback about possible mismatches in question or conditional form may be appropriate: "We wondered about the validity of the assessment task, in light of the specified goal." "If your aim is critical thinking, then the assessments don't seem to us to demand more than recall."

4. Reviewers then give any guidance they might wish to offer in each area where they perceive a gap between intent and effect or confusion about the design's

purpose or execution. Note that guidance should be directed toward improving the designer's intent, not substituting the reviewers' tastes or goals for such a unit.

5. Designer takes notes, asks clarifying questions of reviewers, and thinks out loud about possible implications, as appropriate.

6. After feedback and guidance, discussion by the review group and the designer takes place, covering the general issues and questions raised by the review. A person in the role of recorder takes notes on general design questions, issues, and dilemmas for later discussion by faculty.

Tips for peer review

1. Be prepared to say back to the designer your grasp of the designer's intentions with such clarity and empathy that the person will be completely receptive to any critical feedback and guidance.

2. The reviewers should be friendly, honest consultants (critical friends) to the designer. The designer's intent is the basis of the review. The aim is to improve the designer's idea, not to replace it with the reviewers' teaching priorities, style, or favorite design activities.

3. The designer's job is primarily to listen, not explain, defend, or justify design decisions.

4. The reviewers' job in both sessions is, first, to give useful feedback (*Did the effect match the intent?*); and second, to give useful guidance (*How might the gaps in intent versus effect be removed? How might the design be improved, given the intent?*).

5. Designers typically assume that the design is more self-evident than it is. Imagine yourself to be a naive student or teacher and ponder questions such as these: *Would you know what to do? Would the flow of the unit be obvious? Is it clear what you will be assessed on? Do you see what the purpose of the work is?*

6. Here's the key criterion for judging the success of a peer review: the designer feels that the design was understood by peers and improved (or validated) by the subsequent critique and discussion.

7. Review should always begin by offering feedback in those areas where the design most conforms to the design criteria, describing in detail how and where the design met those criteria.

- "Your task was very authentic; this is clearly the kind of work that a scientist routinely does; the constraints are quite realistic."
- "The unit effectively honors the *W* in WHERETO. By beginning with a study of previous student work on the question and developing rubrics together, it is clear that all students will know what is expected of them in the unit."

8. Giving feedback about problems in the design is always difficult but made easier by casting it more as a conditional response rather than as a firm declaration. Useful phrasings for beginning critical comments in the face-to-face session with the designer include the following:

- "We had a few questions about the validity of...."
- "I had a hard time finding the link between...."
- "We weren't sure about the target...."
- "If your goal was to _____, then I am not seeing so far whether students will be equipped to...."

Avoid saying things that cause defensiveness and resistance, like the following:

- "It was as plain as day to us that this won't work."
- "Your assessment didn't make sense."
- "Kids would never _____."

9. Since the best feedback describes in detail how elements did or did not meet the design criteria, fashion your final written feedback with constant reference to the tests or the criteria listed on the one-page design standards sheet (Figure P.3). A review is not about what you liked or disliked. The designer should be worried about meeting design standards, not about pleasing peers!

10. The most helpful and illuminating discussions (for designers *and* reviewers) tend to focus on considering two questions: (a) To what extent is Stage 1 validly assessed? (b) To what extent does the unit unfold in an engaging and coherent way?

11. Always keep coming back to the alignment of the elements across the three stages, as this is key to good design and often difficult for designers to see well on their own. Consider the following questions:

- Will the assessment plan suit the target and provide valid evidence of the understandings?
- Are *all* targeted understandings, knowledge, and skill addressed by the assessment plan?
- Are *all* the unit questions addressed in the design of the activities and assessments?
- Will the proposed lessons enable successful performance for *all*—especially weaker—students?

Stage 4: Expert Review

By following the UbD peer review process described above, teachers will obtain helpful feedback and guidance from their colleagues to improve their unit designs. However, there are times when unit plans will need a more focused review from a content expert—for example, if the unit topic is relatively esoteric (e.g., ancient history or calculus), if the teacher and peers are generalists, or if the class contains many students with special needs. Expert reviews are also warranted if the unit is being developed for use in a districtwide curriculum (rather than by an individual teacher or school team).

Experts can include fellow teachers or supervisors who have strong expertise on the unit topic, high school subject area teachers, curriculum specialists at the district or regional levels, university professors, and professionals who work in the field. We recommend that all expert reviewers be expected to use the UbD design standards as the basis for providing designer-friendly feedback and guidance.

Design Task: Arrange for peer review or expert review of your draft unit and make any revisions based on the feedback and guidance provided.

Stage 5: Observation by the Designer During Implementation

The rubber meets the road when we implement our unit. The design may meet all of the design standards in the abstract, but the classroom is the proving ground. As the legendary baseball player and philosopher Yogi Berra noted, "You can observe a lot just by watching!" Indeed, we encourage you to pay close attention to the *effect* of your design as you teach it. Here are some questions to consider as you carefully observe and make notes regarding rough spots and needed revisions:

- Which parts of the unit are working well? Which aren't?
- When are students most purposefully engaged? When aren't they? Why?
- Do certain elements of the unit (such as essential questions, performance tasks) work better with some students than others? Why might that be?
- Does the time frame work as planned?
- Are the directions for tasks and activities clear to learners?
- What do the ongoing (formative) assessments reveal about revisions needed for the future?
- What is surprising? Unexpected?
- What adjustments will you make the next time?

Design Tip: Think of the first implementation of your UbD unit as a beta test to observe how users (the students) respond. By carefully observing your students as they work through the unit, you will likely see many elements that need tweaking as students respond in ways other than what you intended or forecasted.

Stage 5: Observation by Outsiders

Visitors to the classroom can provide valuable feedback by offering another set of eyes during implementation of the unit. Administrators, mentors, department chairpersons, team leaders, colleagues, student teachers, or consultants can be enlisted to visit classrooms to observe and provide feedback. We recommend that observations be guided by an agreed-upon set of observable indicators (look-fors), so that feedback is focused on the most salient unit elements and their effect.

Figure P.4 is a general set of observable indicators for use in many classroom situations. You can tailor it to fit your unique situation and use the feedback to consider how effective the unit plays in your classroom.

⟳ **Design Tip:** If possible, arrange for one of more outside observers to visit during the unit's implementation. Agree on a set of observable indicators, listen to their feedback and guidance, and make any revisions that are needed.

Figure P.4

Observable Indicators in the Classroom (General)

Rate the following indicators on the scale of 1= not at all; 2 = infrequently; 3= somewhat; or 4 = greatly.

To what extent are

1. Instruction and assessment focused on big ideas and essential questions based on established standards or outcomes? _____

2. Essential questions revisited throughout a unit? _____

3. Pre-assessments used to check students' prior knowledge and potential misconceptions regarding new topics of study? _____

4. Opening hooks used to engage students in exploring the big ideas and essential questions? _____

5. Students' understanding of the big ideas and core processes assessed through authentic tasks involving one or more of the six facets? _____

6. Evaluations of student products/performances based upon known criteria/rubrics, performance standards, and models (exemplars)? _____

7. Appropriate instructional strategies used to help learners *transfer* their learning, *make meaning* of the big ideas, and *acquire* knowledge and skills? _____

8. Students given regular opportunities to rethink, revise, and reflect on their work based on feedback from ongoing (formative) assessments? _____

9. The students expected to self-assess or reflect on their work and learning and set goals for improvement? _____

10. Other: _____

_____ . _____

Stage 6: Feedback from Results

The point of our unit design is to bring about understanding as reflected in effective performance. Now that the unit has been implemented, we look at the results. To what extent were the desired results, targeted in Stage 1, realized? What does the assessment evidence, identified in Stage 2, reveal about the unit's successes and weaknesses? How effective was the Stage 3 learning plan? Where did students have the most success and why? Where did they struggle most? The performance of students on the unit's assessments and assignments provides specific feedback to inform needed adjustments to the unit design. You can use the self-assessment form in Figure P.5 to consider the strengths and weaknesses and overall effectiveness of the unit.

Figure P.5

Final Self-Assessment Form

UbD Stage 6: Final Unit Assessment Form

Unit _____

Overall unit effectiveness: *ineffective | somewhat effective | effective*
Percent for whom effective: *a few | a minority | a majority | all*
Overall unit engagement: *a few | a minority | a majority | all*

UNIT STRENGTHS: *Check and briefly note any relevant observation:*

    ☐ Students were most successful at _____.
    ☐ Students were most engaged when _____.
    ☐ The Stage 1 elements best achieved were _____.
    ☐ Evidence showed unusually strong results at _____.
    ☐ Even my less able students _____.

UNIT WEAKNESSES: *Check and briefly note any relevant observation:*

    ☐ The unit was not as effective as it might have been, as shown by _____.
    ☐ Students were least successful at _____.
    ☐ Students were least engaged when _____.
    ☐ Stage 1 elements targeted that were not achieved were _____.
    ☐ Evidence showed disappointing results at _____.
    ☐ My less able students had trouble with _____.

Stage 6: Reviewing Student Work in PLC Teams

Although individual teachers certainly can (and do) analyze student work, many educators are encouraged to work in teams or professional learning communities (PLCs) to examine student performance and use the resulting data as a basis for instructional decision making and improvement planning. In cases where two or more teachers implement the same UbD unit, they can look at student work together.

When teachers meet in PLC teams to evaluate the results from common assessments, they begin to identify general patterns of strengths as well as areas needing improvement. We recommend using questions such as the following during a team analysis of student performance:

Evaluate

- What understanding and transfer goals are being assessed?
- What knowledge and skills are being assessed?
- What kinds of thinking are required (e.g., interpretation, problem solving, evaluation)?
- Are these the results I (we) expected? Why or why not?

Given established criteria/rubric(s)

- In what areas did the student(s) perform best?
- What weaknesses are evident?
- What misconceptions are revealed?

Interpret

- What does this work reveal about student understanding and performance?
- What patterns are evident?
- Are these results consistent with other achievement data?
- What questions does this work raise?
- Are there any surprises? Any anomalies?
- Is there evidence of improvement or decline? If so, what caused the changes?
- Are there different possible explanations for these results?

The answers to such questions often lead to specific and effective ideas for improving the unit design.

Stage 6: Feedback from Students

Although students are not experts about the core academic content of the unit, they can often offer the best feedback about what worked and what didn't. They are the "users" of your "software" after all. We strongly encourage you to actively seek feedback from the learners, during and after the unit. Here are some questions to use for that purpose:

- Which parts of the unit best supported your learning? Why?
- Which parts of the unit didn't help you learn? Why?
- Which parts of the unit were most interesting to you?
- Which parts of the unit were least interesting to you?
- What was needlessly frustrating? How might it be improved?
- What do you now really understand as a result of this unit?
- To what extent was the purpose and value of the work clear to you?
- What was surprising? Unexpected?
- What changes would you recommend for the next time this unit is taught?

For older students, you might ask for their feedback and guidance in writing. Alternately, you could interview a sample of students.

Although prompting questions and interviews are a natural way to solicit feedback from learners, some educators use more formal surveys. We have developed such an online survey (see Further Information at end of this module) that can be used to give students opportunities to provide feedback and guidance with respect to the work they are asked to do. Look at these sample answers (with students' original spelling and punctuation intact). What patterns do you notice?

Sample Responses

- The most interesting lesson I had last year was when we made a documentary about the school lunches.
- Learning base 4 in math because i thought that was weird but then i thought well people that dont use base 10 would think thats weird so it made me want to learn other bases as well.
- Poetry. i loved that subject because you get free range to do almost anything with your work
- the most intresting lesson would be in health when we learn about the signs of suicide because it really made me more awre of my suroundings and how it effects our daily lives and i just found that interesting.
- Clay. Definintly Clay. Clay is interesting because it's hands-on, messy, and genuinely your own work. It never end up the way you thought it would.
- Watching sandlot in science and then linking it to experimental design.
- Making the clocks in shop because it was hard and really fun work
- When we were studying conflicts, we would watch little clips of movies and then we had to tell which type of conflict it was.
- The World Religion field trip we took for history. When we went to three different worship places.
- QAR in communication arts it helps me in the reading process.
- The most interesting lesson last year was learning about BizTown in Junior Achievement (simulation of running a business).
  - It was interesting because what we learnt was cool and I knew I was going to be able to use it when we went to BizTown.
  - JA Biztown was the most interesting field trip because we got to be the town people.
  - Biztown was the best experience ever. That was the best because i got to be the CEO of the Children's Hospital.
- Playing bingo in Spanish made it easier to me to learn the vocabulary and made it easier to take tests and quizzes.
- A partner and I went around the room and measured things and recorded to see if they would fit a box. Also we went around the room and wrote down things that had certain angles like right angles and obtuse and acute ones.
- In world history we got to pretend we where on a ship and sailing across the ocean (hallway) on a mission to discover new land. We faced problems on the way. And if we made it we got candy if we died along the way we got nothing.
- when we had to plan and do the notes for a certain chapter. We had to figure out what notes were important, and which people were important.

In the most common answers, students reported that their best learning experiences involved group activities, hands-on work, creative projects, and experiments. Such feedback in the students' own words just might help cautious or habit-bound designers to make some positive changes to their unit designs and learning plans.

⟲ **Design Task:** It is now time to consider all the feedback gathered in Stages 5 and 6, and make whatever adjustments are needed to improve the overall effectiveness of the unit design. Recall that the design-cycle graphic (Figure P.1) portrayed the design and feedback process as an endless loop. Once we have obtained feedback from implementation and results, we start back at the top and consider any new goals or performance gaps that suggest needed or desired revisions to the unit.

Self-Assessment—Review Criteria for Module P

Now that you have thought about the details of lesson planning, it's time to conduct a careful self-assessment of your design. Is it ready to be implemented successfully?

- Do I understand the design criteria, and can I comfortably self-assess my unit in Stage 4? Have I self-assessed my unit against the design criteria and rubrics with a disciplined look at what might need improvement?
- Have I made sufficient attempts to get feedback on my unit—from colleagues, from students, and from outside experts?
- Do I understand the UbD peer review protocols provided, and have I taken steps to find colleagues to engage in peer review together?
- Do I understand the "look-fors" in Stage 5 as the unit is under way? Have I become better at analyzing the unit's strengths and weaknesses as distinguished from my teaching or the students' behavior?
- Do I understand how to analyze the results from the unit in Stage 6? Am I comfortable analyzing work products and test results in order to improve the unit in the future?

🖱 Online you'll find many additional forms and worksheets to help you obtain feedback from various sources: Figure P.6, Observable Indicators in the Classroom (Learner Focused); Figure P.7, Detailed Rubric for UbD Design Standards 2.0; Figure P.8, Final Self-Assessment Form Based on Feedback; Figure P.9, Peer Review—Individual or Group Review Form; Figure P.10, UbD Stage 4/5 Visit Planner; Figure P.11, UbD Stage 5 Observation Form; Figure P.12, UbD Stage 5 Understanding "Look-Fors"—Transfer; Figure P.13: UbD Stage 5 Understanding "Look-Fors"—Meaning; Figure P.14, Unit Design Tips and Guidelines.

Further Information on the Ideas and Issues in This Module

Online student survey is available through www.authenticeducation.org. Look for the link to the student survey. Results of the survey are also available.

Schooling by Design: Mission, Action, and Achievement (Wiggins & McTighe, 2007). Chapters 6–7. These two chapters (on "What Is My Job?") argue for the importance of peer review and review of student work as a central role of educators. In fact, we propose that these tasks be made part of the formal contractual obligation.

Understanding by Design: Professional Development Workbook (McTighe & Wiggins, 2004). Pages 242–248 provide further detail on the peer review process and additional forms that can be used when following the protocol.

References

McTighe, J., & Wiggins, G. (2004). *Understanding by Design: Professional development workbook*. Alexandria, VA: ASCD.

Wiggins, G., & McTighe, J. (2007). *Schooling by design: Mission, action, and achievement*. Alexandria, VA: ASCD.

Wiggins, G., & McTighe, J. (2011). *The Understanding by Design guide to creating high-quality units*. Alexandria, VA: ASCD.

Conclusion

Congratulations on completing this *Guide*! No doubt you'll agree that UbD unit design is challenging work. Nonetheless, we trust that the tools, tips, exercises, and examples have been helpful. In this concluding section, we offer tips for moving forward with UbD and cautionary notes to help you avoid unintentionally undermining your efforts.

Tips for Moving Forward

Start small. As with any other skill, practice in designing units will improve your ability and efficiency. In fact, if you keep at it, we predict that your experience will parallel that of thousands of other teachers who have found that UbD unit design becomes a way of thinking. However, we caution against trying to plan *everything* you teach using UbD, at least at first. Because this design process is demanding, we recommend planning two or three units a year as a start. Then expand to additional units in future years.

Work collaboratively. If possible, work with a colleague or two when planning UbD units. Most designers find it valuable to bounce ideas around during design, give each other feedback along the way, and examine student work together. Once you and your teammates get the hang of it, you can "work smarter" by dividing up the planning work among department or grade-level teams; perhaps you take the lead in developing Units 1 and 3, while your teammate plans Units 2 and 4. Then you share.

Think big. As you now know, the *Guide* has focused on designing units of study within which individual lessons are planned. However, you may have wondered: If we truly apply backward design, wouldn't it make sense to design the overall curriculum and courses *before* units and lessons? Well, yes. In an ideal world, unit designers would be able to draw upon overarching elements (transfer goals, understandings, essential questions, cornerstone assessments, and multigrade rubrics) that had already been established at the programmatic, departmental, and course levels. Indeed, that is the approach to district and school curriculum planning that we advocate and describe in *Schooling by Design* (Wiggins & McTighe, 2007).

However, our experience in introducing the understanding by design framework to teacher-designers favors the Goldilocks approach; that is, begin in a design space that is just right: bigger than a daily lesson but smaller than a year-long curriculum.

Once you become comfortable planning at the unit level, it makes sense to think bigger and map the entire year using UbD elements. Indeed, this is a natural evolution for school teams as well as district curriculum committees.

Plan to adjust based on results. As noted in Module P, unit design is a means to an end—engaging and effective learning. Consequently, the most effective teachers constantly monitor the effects of their designs, along the way through formative assessments and at the conclusion by analyzing student performance. We recommend that you get in the habit of planning adjustments to your design (during and after) in real time. Working with electronic design templates makes ongoing revision a natural part of the overall process.

How Not to "Kill" UbD

We end on a cautionary note, suggested by the section title. Alas, too many well-meaning administrators and enthusiastic teachers have unwittingly killed UbD instead of helping it flourish and grow. Here are six potential problems with corresponding recommendations for avoiding them:

Ways to Kill UbD from the Start	Ways to Nurture UbD
1. Mandate that all teachers must use UbD for *all* of their planning immediately (without sufficient training, ongoing support, or structured planning time).	1. Think big, but start small: • Work with volunteers at first. • Ask all teachers to plan one unit per semester to start. • Encourage teachers to work with a colleague or team, and begin with a familiar unit topic. • Provide some designated planning time.
2. Introduce UbD as *this* year's focus (suggesting that UbD can be fully implemented in a year and that last year's initiative bears no relation to it). This approach fosters a "this too shall pass" attitude among staff.	2. Develop and publish a multiyear plan that shows how UbD will be slowly yet systematically implemented as part of a strategic plan.

Ways to Kill UbD from the Start	Ways to Nurture UbD
3. Attempt to implement too many initiatives *simultaneously* (e.g., UbD, differentiated instruction, curriculum mapping, and professional learning communities).	3. Develop a multistage, multiyear plan to improve a current initiative via UbD; for example: • Curriculum mapping • Differentiation via essential questions and authentic tasks • Unpacking standards via "big ideas" Develop a one-page graphic showing how all initiatives are really interconnected parts of an overall effort (using analogies such as the limbs of a tree, pieces of a puzzle, supports of a building).
4. Assume that staff members understand the need for UbD or will naturally welcome it.	4. Establish the need for a change (the diagnosis) before proposing UbD as the prescription. Make sure that staff see UbD as an appropriate response to a need they recognize and own.
5. Provide one introductory presentation on UbD and assume that teachers can implement UbD well.	5. Design professional development backward from your goals. Build a year with design workshops, study groups, and action research, during which staff go through many cycles of learning, trying, and getting feedback and then adjusting according to feedback.
6. Offer UbD training for teachers but not for administrators. Conversely, administrators and supervisors need the same training as teachers.	6. Establish parallel tracks of training for administrators in which they learn how to supervise and support UbD—for example, how to conduct in-class look-fors, establish peer reviews of units, form PLC teams to analyze assessment results.

References

Wiggins, G., & McTighe, J. (2007). *Schooling by design.* Alexandria, VA: ASCD.

About the Authors

 **Grant Wiggins** is president of Authentic Education in Hopewell, New Jersey. He earned his EdD from Harvard University and his BA from St. John's College in Annapolis. Grant and his colleagues consult with schools, districts, and state and national education departments on a variety of reform matters. He and his colleagues also organize conferences and workshops, and develop print and web resources on key school reform issues.

Grant is perhaps best known for being coauthor, with Jay McTighe, of *Understanding by Design*, the award-winning and highly successful program and set of materials on curriculum design used all over the world, and of *Schooling by Design*. He is also a coauthor for Pearson Publishing on more than a dozen textbook programs in which UbD is infused. His work has been supported by the Pew Charitable Trusts, the Geraldine R. Dodge Foundation, and the National Science Foundation.

For 25 years, Grant has worked on influential reform initiatives around the world, including Ted Sizer's Coalition of Essential Schools; the International Baccalaureate Program; the Advanced Placement Program; state reform initiatives in New Jersey, New York, and Delaware; and national reforms in China, the Philippines, and Thailand.

Grant is widely known for his work in assessment reform. He is the author of *Educative Assessment* and *Assessing Student Performance*, both published by Jossey-Bass. He was a lead consultant on many state assessment reform initiatives, such as the portfolio project in Vermont and performance assessment consortia in New Jersey and North Carolina.

Several journals have published Grant's articles, including *Educational Leadership* and *Phi Delta Kappan*. His work is grounded in 14 years of secondary school teaching and coaching. Grant taught English and electives in philosophy, coached varsity soccer and cross country, as well as junior varsity baseball and track and field. He also plays in the Hazbins, a rock band. Grant may be contacted at gwiggins@authenticeducation.org.

 **Jay McTighe** brings a wealth of experience developed during a rich and varied career in education. He served as director of the Maryland Assessment Consortium, a state collaboration of school districts working together to develop and share formative performance assessments. Prior to this position, Jay was involved with school improvement projects at the Maryland State Department of Education where he directed the development of the Instructional Framework, a multimedia database on teaching. Jay is well known for his work with thinking skills, having coordinated statewide efforts to develop instructional strategies, curriculum models, and assessment procedures for improving the quality of student thinking. In addition to his work at the state level, Jay has experience at the district level in Prince George's County, Maryland, as a classroom teacher, resource specialist, and program coordinator. He also directed a state residential enrichment program for gifted and talented students.

Jay is an accomplished author, having coauthored 10 books, including the best-selling *Understanding by Design* series with Grant Wiggins. He has written more than 30 articles and book chapters, and has published in leading journals, including *Educational Leadership* (ASCD) and *The Developer* (National Staff Development Council).

Jay has an extensive background in professional development and is a regular speaker at national, state, and district conferences and workshops. He has made presentations in 47 states within the United States, in 7 Canadian provinces, and 18 other countries on 5 continents.

Jay received his undergraduate degree from the College of William and Mary, earned his master's degree from the University of Maryland, and completed postgraduate studies at the Johns Hopkins University. He was selected to participate in the Educational Policy Fellowship Program through the Institute for Educational Leadership in Washington, D.C., and served as a member of the National Assessment Forum, a coalition of education and civil rights organizations advocating reforms in national, state, and local assessment policies and practices. Contact information: Jay McTighe, 6581 River Run, Columbia, MD 21044-6066 USA. E-mail: jmctigh@aol.com.

At the time of publication, the following ASCD resources were available (ASCD stock numbers appear in parentheses). For up-to-date information about ASCD resources, go to www.ascd.org.

ASCD EDge Group

Exchange ideas and connect with other educators interested in Understanding by Design on the social networking site ASCD EDge® at http://ascdedge.ascd.org/ or log onto ASCD's website at www.ascd.org and click on Research a Topic.

Print Products

Integrating Differentiated Instruction and Understanding by Design: Connecting Content and Kids Carol Ann Tomlinson and Jay McTighe (#105004)

Making the Most of Understanding by Design John L. Brown (#103110)

Schooling by Design: An ASCD Action Tool (#707039)

Schooling by Design: Mission, Action, and Achievement Grant Wiggins and Jay McTighe (#107018)

Understanding by Design Expanded 2nd edition Grant Wiggins and Jay McTighe (#103055)

The Understanding by Design Guide to Creating High-Quality Units Grant Wiggins and Jay McTighe (#109107)

The Understanding by Design Professional Development Workbook Jay McTighe and Grant Wiggins (#103056)

DVDs

Connecting Differentiated Instruction, Understanding by Design, and What Works in Schools: An Exploration of Research-Based Strategies with Carol Ann Tomlinson, Jay McTighe, Grant Wiggins, and Robert J. Marzano (#609012)

THE WHOLE CHILD The Whole Child Initiative helps schools and communities create learning environments that allow students to be healthy, safe, engaged, supported, and challenged. To learn more about other books and resources that relate to the whole child, visit www.wholechildeducation.org.

For more information: send e-mail to member@ascd.org; call 1-800-933-2723 or 703-578-9600, press 2; send a fax to 703-575-5400; or write to Information Services, ASCD, 1703 N. Beauregard St., Alexandria, VA 22311-1714 USA.